CATCH MORE FISH

A STEP-BY-STEP APPROACH
TO FISHING SUCCESS

SHADY OAK PRESS

RIVERHEAD FREE LIBRARY
330 COURT ST
RIVERHEAD, NY 11901

D1192076

Catch More Fish
A Step-by-Step Approach to Fishing Success

All rights reserved. No part of this publication may be reproduced, stored in an electronic retrieval system or transmitted in any form or by any means (electronic, mechanical, photocopying, recording or otherwise) without the prior written permission of the copyright owner.

Tom Carpenter
Creative Director

Jen Weaverling
Managing Editor

Wendy Holdman
Senior Book Designer

Greg Schweiters
Cover Design

Michele Teigen
Senior Book Development Coordinator

Bill Lindner, Tom Heck, Mike Hehner, Dick Sternberg
Photography

Dave Schelitzche and Joe Tomelleri
Illustration

Julie Cisler
Book Design & Production

Dick Sternberg has combined his skills as a biologist and multi-species angler to write over 20 books on freshwater fishing.

1 2 3 4 5 6 / 13 12 11 10 09 08
©1998 North American Membership Group
ISBN: 978-1-58159-365-5

Distributed by:
Sterling Publishing Co., Inc.
387 Park Avenue South
New York, NY 10016-8810

For information about custom editions, special sales, premium and corporate purchases, please contact Sterling Special Sales Department at 800-805-5489 or specialsales@sterlingpublishing.com.

Printed in China

SHADY OAK PRESS

12301 Whitewater Drive
Minnetonka, MN 55343

CONTENTS

INTRODUCTION

*C*atch More Fish will help you become a better angler, and not because it focuses on the hottest new lure or the latest breakthroughs in fishing electronics. Rather, it highlights the habits of the gamefish you target in the waters you fish. After all, the key to consistently successful angling is finding fish. Even the best lure made can't catch a fish that isn't there!

No matter if you fish bass, salmon, walleye or any other species of fish, or if you are a beginning angler or an expert, *Catch More Fish* contains the information you need to plan a successful fishing strategy. Its clear, concise text and easy-to-understand color photographs are sure to make you a more versatile, more successful angler.

Tom Carpenter
Shady Oak Press

UNDERSTANDING FRESHWATER GAMEFISH

The first step to becoming a successful angler is developing a basic understanding of the fish you're trying to catch. Without this knowledge, even the most expensive equipment will do you no good.

You don't have to be a fisheries biologist in order to consistently catch fish, but it helps to be aware of your quarry's strongest senses, its feeding habits and the habitat it prefers. And that's what we cover here.

GAMEFISH SENSES

Walleyes and other gamefish can detect prey that they cannot see by picking up vibrations with their lateral line (dotted line).

Every gamefish species is equipped with a set of senses that enables it to survive in an ever-changing aquatic world. When the water is clear, for example, most fish rely heavily on vision to find food and avoid predators, including fishermen. But, when the water suddenly turns muddy from a heavy rain, they depend mainly on hearing and their lateral-line system.

Although every gamefish species has each of the senses we are about to discuss, the acuity of specific senses varies considerably among species. Although there have been no broad-scope studies to quantify these differences, there have been some studies on particular fish. And, from visual observation, we also know which senses are important to many species. These differences will be discussed in the chapter on "Fishing Techniques" (p.74).

Vision

In all gamefish, the retina of the eye is equipped with both rods (intensity receptors) and cones (color receptors). The cone-to-rod ratio is highest in shallow-water species, such as bass and sunfish, meaning that they have better color vision than deep-water species. Researchers believe that most shallow-water fish see the same range of colors as humans.

Good color vision would be virtually meaningless to fish in deep water, because water acts as a color filter. Red is filtered out at a depth of only 10 feet and yellow disappears at about 20. Blue may be visible at depths of 50 feet or more, assuming there is adequate light penetration. But even if fish can't see the color of an object, they may recognize it as a shade of gray. This explains why most veteran anglers place more importance on the flash, action and size of a lure than on the exact color.

Fish that have good color vision may not have good night vision, however, because the retina does not have enough rods. The northern pike falls into this category. Some gamefish, like Pacific salmon, are capable of switching from cone to rod vision as light levels fade.

How far and how clearly a fish can see depends more on water clarity than visual acuity. In very clear water, most gamefish can easily see 75 feet or more. In highly turbid water, they would be hard-pressed to see a foot.

Lateral Line

This sense, not present in humans, enables fish to pick up vibrations in the water that help them detect predators, prey and even anglers' lures.

The lateral line consists of a row of pores along each side of the fish, extending from the gill to the base of the tail. The pores are connected to a network of nerve endings that sense the slightest vibrations and transmit them to receptors in the inner ear.

Using its lateral line, a fish can determine not only if predators or prey are present, but how big they are, how fast they're moving and in what direction. The lateral line also helps schools of fish swim in unison.

Hearing

Fish do not have external ears, but they have inner ears, which consist of tiny bones that pick up sound and semi-circular canals that help maintain equilibrium. They do not have an ear drum, however, so vibrations are sent to the ear through body tissues.

Many anglers, knowing that gamefish can detect underwater sounds, use lures with rattles when fishing after dark or in murky water.

Smell/Taste

Most gamefish have an acute sense of smell and are

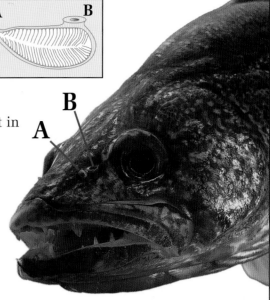

To detect odors, fish take in water through (A) incurrent nares. It passes through the nasal capsule where odors are picked up by folds of sensory tissue (cutaway). The water is then expelled through (B) excurrent nares.

able to detect the odor of nearby predators and prey, assuming the current is favorable. But some gamefish rely on scent much more than others. Scent is most important in catfish, trout, salmon and sunfish, and least important in bass, walleyes and pike.

This explains why catfish anglers have so much success with "stinkbait," why fresh spawn works so well for trout and salmon, and why scented soft-plastics catch so many sunfish. Scented baits are much less effective on other gamefish.

In most gamefish, the sense of taste is much less significant than the sense of smell. But bullheads and catfish do use their sense of taste, especially in muddy water. They comb the bottom, using taste buds in their whiskers and on their skin to find food.

Eyes positioned on the side of the head and toward the top make it possible for fish to see in every direction, except straight behind them and below them.

FOOD & FEEDING HABITS

Anglers are constantly trying to determine why gamefish behave the way they do. Practically everyone who wets a line has a theory involving wind direction, cloud cover, water temperature, water pH, moon phase or dozens of other factors. But the number-one factor influencing the daily lives of gamefish is food.

A gamefish will endure water well outside its preferred temperature or pH range, and even will venture into water with practically no dissolved oxygen, if that water holds the food it wants.

Although every fish has a preference for certain foods, those foods may not be available at all times. If a gamefish is to survive, it must learn to be an opportunist.

This explains why the diet of most gamefish changes several times over the course of a year, depending on the abundance of particular food items. To catch fish consistently, you must learn how food availability can affect gamefish behavior.

If bass are busting into schools of shad in open water, for example, you may be able to catch them on topwaters. But when they're rooting crayfish out of the rocks, a jig would be a much better choice.

In most cases, it is not necessary to use a lure that looks precisely like the food the fish are eating. But it helps to select a lure of about the same size with a similar type of action.

Differences in food availability also explain why gamefish in one body of water can behave much differently than those in another. For instance, walleyes in a lake where perch are the primary food do most of their feeding on deep structure, because that's where most of the perch are found. But where shad or ciscoes are the main food, walleyes spend much more time cruising open water.

Common Feeding Behaviors

Ambush predators, such as muskies, lie in wait in dense cover, waiting for baitfish or other foods to make a mistake and come too close. Then, they attack with a burst of speed and return to their resting spot to digest their meal.

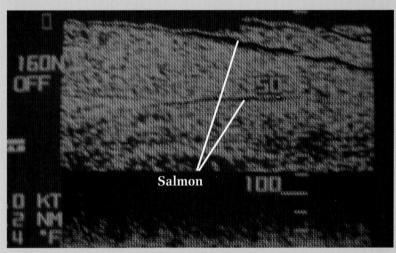

Salmon

Open water feeders, such as chinook salmon, go wherever they must to find schools of baitfish. This video screen shows a cloud of alewives with several chinooks in its midst.

Scavengers, such as channel catfish, comb the bottom for any kind of food they can find. They will take live crayfish, mussels, insect larvae and baitfish, but will also eat dead or rotting organic material.

Larval aquatic insects are one of the most important foods for young gamefish and, in some cases, adults. During a heavy insect hatch, gamefish like trout and walleyes may feed exclusively on a particular kind of insect larvae.

Tiny mollusks (snails and clams) are food for many kinds of juvenile gamefish. Larger mollusks are food for bottom feeders like catfish. Snails make up a large part of the diet of redear sunfish, accounting for their common name, shellcracker.

Crustaceans are an important food source for all sizes of gamefish. Young fish graze on tiny crustaceans called scuds (shown), while larger fish eat crustaceans like grass shrimp and crayfish.

Small fish make up the majority of the diet of adult bass, walleye, pike and other large predators. As a rule, long, thin fish like shiners make better forage than deep-bodied fish like sunfish, because they slide down easier.

Large fish like adult suckers, whitefish and even rainbow trout are the preferred food of big pike, muskies, lake trout, bass and other good-sized predators. By eating one large fish instead of several small ones, they conserve energy. This 6-pound lake trout has battle scars from a previous encounter with a 40-pound-plus laker.

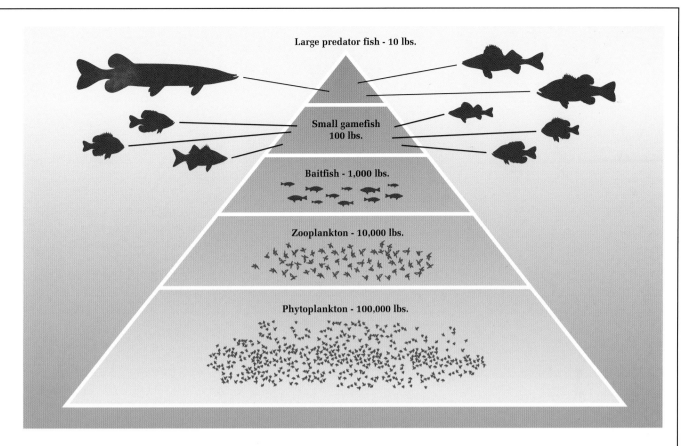

Large predator fish - 10 lbs.

Small gamefish
100 lbs.

Baitfish - 1,000 lbs.

Zooplankton - 10,000 lbs.

Phytoplankton - 100,000 lbs.

Understanding the Food Pyramid

The abundance of gamefish in any body of water is dependent on the abundance of plankton. Without enough phytoplankton, for instance, there wouldn't be enough zooplankton to feed the baitfish, and without enough baitfish, there would be a shortage of gamefish.

Many biologists talk about these food relationships in terms of a food chain, which basically shows what eats what.

But a food pyramid is a more meaningful concept, because it shows how much of each type of food is needed to produce how many pounds of top-rung predators. Although the exact percentage varies greatly depending on the situation, the poundage produced at each level of the pyramid is only about 10 percent of the level below it. In the above example, 100,000 pounds of phytoplankton produce only 10 pounds of large predator fish.

Feeding Triggers

Insect hatches may cause fish to suddenly start feeding. Fish know that a hatch lasts only for a short time, and they must move quickly to get an easy meal.

Approaching storms cause a rapid decrease in light level and a drop in barometric pressure, which may initiate a feeding spree.

Wind pounding into a shoreline creates a mudline. Windblown plankton draws baitfish and, in turn, gamefish that can feed comfortably in low-light conditions.

FISH HABITAT

Walleyes deposit their eggs along windswept rubble shorelines. The eggs slip into crevices in the rocks where wave action keeps them aerated and prevents them from silting over and suffocating.

spawning, the proper range of water temperature, adequate dissolved oxygen and a reliable supply of food. Without any one of these elements, long-term survival would be impossible.

If you take time to study the habitat needs of gamefish, catching them becomes much easier. You'll not only know where to look, but where not to look.

Spawning Habitat

The spawning habits of gamefish vary greatly and so does their spawning-habitat needs. Northern pike, for instance, can spawn successfully in shallow, marshy bays, but if walleyes attempted to spawn there, the eggs would probably not survive.

Shown on this page are a few of the many habitats used by spawning gamefish. You'll learn more details in the chapter, "Fishing Techniques" (p.74).

Every kind of gamefish has its own unique habitat requirements. Even closely related species, like smallmouth and largemouth bass, have a slightly different set of habitat preferences. In order to target a particular species of fish, you must understand its habitat needs.

The term, habitat, means the combination of environmental elements that a fish needs to survive. For gamefish, that combination includes the right kind of cover, good conditions for

Types of Spawning Habitat

A hard, sandy bottom with emergent vegetation, such as bulrushes, for cover, makes ideal spawning habitat for sunfish, crappies and other panfish, especially when it is in a bay or along a sheltered shoreline.

Trout and salmon dig their redds in gravel beds in flowing water. The eggs are deposited in the depression, then covered with gravel. Water flowing through the gravel keeps the eggs oxygenated.

Hiding cover provides young fish protection from a host of aquatic and avian predators. Common types of hiding cover include dense weeds and brush, crevices between rocks, docks, piers and other man-made cover.

Gamefish Cover

Without some type of cover, the life expectancy of a newly hatched fish could be measured in minutes. The tiny hatchling, or fry, would soon become an easy meal for an aquatic predator, such as a minnow, a crayfish or, possibly, an insect. If it is lucky enough to survive for a few weeks and grow a little larger, it attracts predators like bass, herons, grebes and turtles that are looking for a more sub-stantial meal. This intense predation explains why less than one percent of the fish that hatch ever see adulthood.

All but the largest gamefish are also subject to predation, but they need cover for other reasons, as well. Cover provides shade, protection from the current and a hiding spot from which to ambush prey. And, in the heat of summer, overhead cover keeps the water a little cooler.

Ambush cover conceals predator fish so they can dart out and grab unsuspecting prey. Most predators avoid thick weeds or other dense cover because they cannot maneuver well enough.

Overhead cover protects fish from avian predators, provides shade and may keep the water slightly cooler. Common types include undercut banks, root wads and beds of floating-leaf vegetation.

Nesting cover, such as boulders and logs, makes it easier for nesting fish to guard their eggs and newly hatched fry, because the nest is protected on at least one side.

Shelter from current is a must for most fish that live in moving water. This explains why they seek cover in eddies that form downstream of boulders, log jams, bridge piers, islands and points.

Water Temperature

Although fish are cold-blooded, different species have distinctly different water-temperature preferences. Biologists place gamefish in three temperature categories. Coldwater fish (trout and salmon), prefer water temperatures in the 50s; coolwater fish (pike, muskie, walleye, sauger and perch), in the 60s; and warmwater fish (bass, crappies, sunfish, catfish), 70 to 80.

But just because a fish prefers a certain temperature doesn't mean it will always be found in water of that temperature. Fish go where they must to find food, and even a major difference in water temperature won't stop them.

In summer, when oxygen levels sag in deep water, coldwater fish are forced into shallower water, where oxygen levels are higher. They are under some stress, but they can usually endure it until the water starts to cool in fall.

Some coldwater fish can tolerate water well above their preferred temperature range. Brown trout, for example, prefer water of about 58 to 62°F, but they're sometimes found in the lower reaches of streams where the water is in the upper 70s.

Conversely, most warmwater fish can tolerate very cold water. Sunfish, crappies and bass live in many waters that ice over in winter, and they continue to feed at near-freezing temperatures.

But, as a rule, the greater the difference between a fish's preferred temperature range and the actual water temperature, the less active it is likely to be. The brown trout in the warm stream, for instance, will be difficult to catch because it is feeding very little. The same

holds true for the bass in the frozen lake.

As gamefish grow older, they generally prefer cooler water. This pattern is most evident in northern pike. Small pike like water in the 67- to 72-degree range, but

once they reach 30 inches in length (about 7 pounds), they prefer 50- to 55-degree water. Their preference for cooler water explains why large fish are generally found in deeper water than small ones.

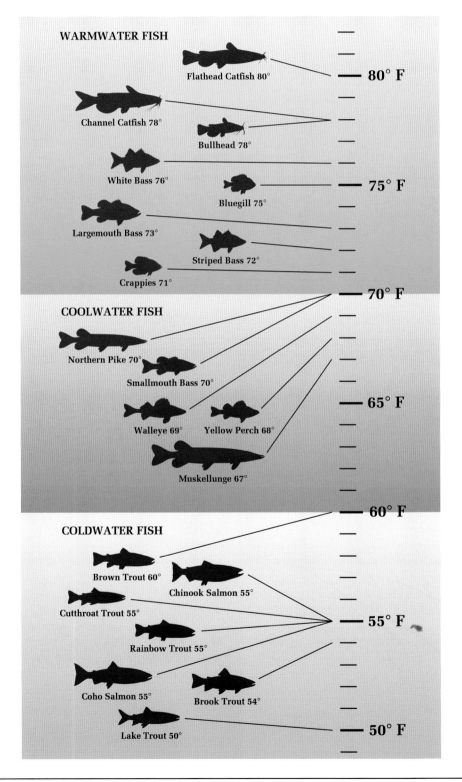

The Fall Turnover

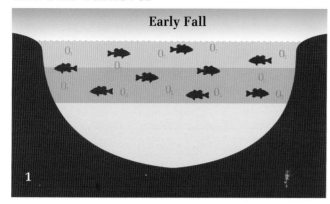

Early Fall

1

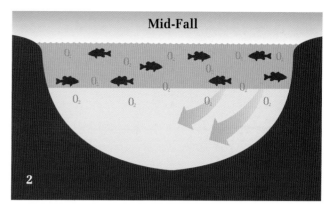

Mid-Fall

2

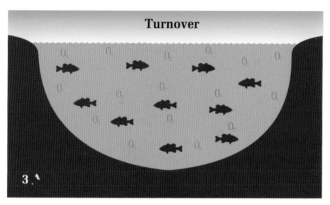

Turnover

3.

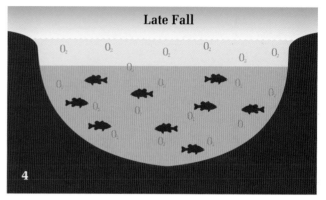

Late Fall

4

(1) In early fall, the lake is still stratified into three temperature layers. Fish are found only in the upper two layers, because oxygen levels are too low in the hypolimnion. (2) As the upper layer cools in mid-fall, the surface water starts to sink and (3) the turnover begins, scattering fish to all depths. (4) By late fall, the surface water is cooler than the water on the bottom, so practically all of the fish are deep.

Stratification & Turnover

Water is densest at a temperature of 39.2°F. As it gets warmer or colder, it becomes less dense. This density difference causes most lakes to stratify into temperature layers. The deepest, coldest, densest layer is called the *hypolimnion;* the shallowest, warmest, lightest layer, the *epilimnion.* Between the two is a zone called the *thermocline,* where the temperature changes rapidly.

The warmer, lighter water in the epilimnion floats on top of the cooler, heavier water in the depths. And because the water is lighter, it is more easily circulated by the wind. The thermocline may have slight water circulation, but the water below it circulates very little.

After a lake stratifies in early summer, a stagnation process begins. Decaying organic material on the lake bottom, along with living organisms in the water, consume dissolved oxygen. With no circulation to restore it and no aquatic plants to produce it, oxygen levels in the hypolimnion begin to decline. Just how fast they decline depends on the water fertility (p.16).

The temperature layers remain intact through the summer, as long as the weather is warm enough to keep the surface water several degrees warmer than the water in the depths. But when the weather cools

enough that the shallows reach the same temperature as the depths, the fall turnover begins. Because all of the water in the lake is now at the same temperature and density, the wind can circulate the entire water mass. As the surface continues to cool, the water becomes denser than that in the depths so it sinks vertically, bolstering the mixing process.

Mixing from top to bottom continues through the fall. In the North, the surface freezes, but the water on the bottom stays several degrees above freezing. If water did not have the unusual property of being densest at a temperature slightly above freezing, lakes would freeze completely to the bottom.

Eutrophic lakes are shallow and weedy, with highly fertile water. A heavy algae bloom usually develops in summer. These lakes are best suited for warmwater gamefish and roughfish.

Water Fertility

The term "water fertility" refers to the amount of nutrients, such as nitrogen and phosphorus, dissolved in the water. A body of water with high fertility is said to be *eutrophic;* moderate fertility, *mesotrophic;* and low fertility, *oligotrophic.*

Fertility, in itself, has little effect on the daily lives of gamefish. If all of their other habitat requirements are met, they can live in water of most any fertility level.

But fertility is the major determinant of how many pounds of fish a body of water can produce. Just as the amount of fertilizer you spread on your lawn determines how fast your grass will grow, the level of dissolved nutrients in the water determines how much phytoplankton (p.11) is produced and, thus, how much food is available to gamefish. That, in turn, affects their growth rate and, ultimately, the poundage of fish the body of water can support.

Oligotrophic lakes are generally deep, clear and infertile, with sparse weed growth. They are best suited for coolwater and coldwater gamefish, although shallow bays may hold warmwater species.

Mesotrophic lakes usually have moderate depth, water clarity, water fertility and weed growth. These lakes often support warmwater and coolwater gamefish.

Fertility has yet another indirect influence on gamefish. It is the primary factor determining the level of dissolved oxygen in the water (opposite) so it controls where fish can live and where they cannot.

Dissolved Oxygen

Fish vary greatly in their dissolved oxygen (D.O.) needs. While some species, like bullheads, can get by with practically no oxygen, others, such as trout, require a great deal.

Oxygen levels are measured in parts per million (ppm). When water is fully saturated with oxygen, the D.O. level is about 10 ppm, depending on the water temperature.

You may have noticed that fish are much easier to keep alive in your livewell when the water is cold. There are two reasons for this: Fish in cold water require less oxygen, and the water can hold more oxygen.

Oxygen gets into the water through contact with the air and photosynthesis by aquatic plants. It is consumed by respiration of aquatic organisms ranging from bacteria to gamefish.

In fertile lakes, organic matter is so plentiful that oxygen is consumed faster than it is replenished. In summer, when a lake stratifies, the layer of decaying organic ooze on the bottom rapidly consumes oxygen and, with no circulation to replace it, oxygen levels wane, forcing fish into shallower water.

The fall turnover replenishes oxygen levels, but they begin to dip again in winter. If snow and ice cover are heavy enough to prevent sunlight penetration, plants cannot produce oxygen through photosynthesis, so oxygen levels plummet. If they plummet far enough, fish begin to die and the lake is said to freeze out, or *winterkill.*

Summer oxygen depletion or winterkill are not a problem in infertile lakes, because oxygen is consumed much more slowly.

Minimum Wintertime Oxygen Tolerances of Freshwater Fish Species	
Trout	3ppm
Bass	2ppm
Catfish	2ppm
Sunfish	2ppm
Walleye	2ppm
Muskies	2ppm
White Bass/Stripers	1.5ppm
Crappies	1.5ppm
Perch	1.5ppm
Northern pike	1ppm
Carp	1ppm
Bullheads	.5ppm

How Dissolved Oxygen is Replenished

Oxygen enters the water through contact with the air. Wind circulates the water, carrying oxygen to fish in the depths. In summer, however, the lower layer does not circulate, so no oxygen is added.

When the leaves of plants are exposed to sunlight, oxygen is produced through the process of photosynthesis. When sunlight cannot reach the plants, no oxygen is produced.

FISHING WATERS

To become a successful angler, you must learn what kind of waters hold what kind of fish and why.

Whether you fish natural lakes, man-made lakes or rivers and streams, the pages that follow will show you the types of waters best suited to your favorite type of fishing.

NATURAL LAKES

The Great Lakes, because of their huge size and great depth, stay cold throughout the year, so they support a variety of trout and salmon. But there are many shallow bays and some shallower basins, such as the western basin of Lake Erie, that are warm enough to support warmwater and coolwater fish, like smallmouth bass and walleyes.

Natural lakes include everything from sink holes covering only a few acres to the vast inland seas called the Great Lakes. But these waters have one thing in common: practically all of them hold gamefish.

Scientists who study natural lakes do not agree on how many different types there are or how they should be categorized. Some say there are more than 100 kinds of lakes. But none of this means much to freshwater anglers; they're more concerned about the species and number of fish a lake produces.

From a fisherman's standpoint, there are really only three main categories of freshwater lakes: warmwater lakes, which support warmwater gamefish; coldwater lakes, which support trout, salmon and other coldwater species, like ciscoes and whitefish; and two-story lakes, which support both warmwater and coldwater species. Within each of these categories are lakes of different sizes, shapes and fertility levels.

Warmwater lakes, by far the most numerous type, are found throughout North America, with the exception of the Far North. There, the summers are so short that the water never gets much above 60°F.

Coldwater lakes, the rarest type, exist only in the Far North, in mountainous regions, or where there is enough spring flow to keep the water cold in summer.

Many warmwater lakes have a layer of deep, cold water but, in most cases, this water lacks sufficient dissolved oxygen, so they are not considered two-story lakes. Only those whose depths contain adequate oxygen in summer qualify as two-story lakes.

On these pages are a few of the wide variety of natural lakes found in North America.

Arctic lakes, because of the short summers, stay cold throughout the year. Primarily lake trout producers, many of these lakes also have good numbers of pike and grayling.

Alpine lakes are fed by snowmelt and, because they are at high altitudes, stay cold throughout the year. They support a variety of trout species.

Walleye lakes have sandy shorelines with moderate weed growth. They support a variety of species including bass, panfish, perch, walleyes, pike and, quite often, muskies.

Bass-panfish lakes have mucky shorelines with a few sandy areas and heavy weed growth. They hold largemouth bass, sunfish, crappies, northern pike and numerous kinds of roughfish.

Canadian-shield lakes, because of their bedrock basins, usually have low fertility levels. Many are true two-story lakes, with walleyes, pike and smallmouth in the shallows and lake trout in the depths.

Freeze-out lakes periodically winterkill. They usually hold large numbers of bullheads and other roughfish that are tolerant of low oxygen. But, when there are several years between winterkills, they produce largemouth bass, panfish and pike.

MAN-MADE LAKES

Man-made lakes, also called *reservoirs* or *impoundments*, are created by damming creeks, streams or big rivers. They serve several purposes, including flood control, supplying water for municipalities, irrigating crops and generating electric power.

The size, shape and depth of the lake that is formed depends on the terrain and the height of the dam.

Man-made lakes differ from natural lakes in that the water level usually fluctuates much more. In many reservoirs, the water is drawn down in fall to make room for spring runoff. Some reservoirs fluctuate more than 50 feet over the course of the year.

With the water level changing this much, fish are forced to move much more than they would in a natural lake. A creek arm that held good numbers of bass in spring, for instance, may be completely dry in fall, so the fish have no choice but to move out. The changing water level also makes it difficult for aquatic plants to gain a foothold.

Man-made lakes, like natural lakes, usually stratify into temperature layers. But, in bottom-draw reservoirs,

Lowland reservoirs, often located in swampy areas, are seldom more than 25 feet deep. These highly fertile, low-clarity waters lack distinct creek arms. They usually hold largemouth bass, sunfish, crappies and catfish.

the layer of cold water on the bottom is thinner, because of the deep-water discharge. The coldwater draw may allow trout to live in the river downstream of the reservoir.

Unlike natural lakes, reservoirs seldom winterkill, because the inflow maintains adequate oxygen levels.

The life of a reservoir is considerably shorter than that of a natural lake. The silt load carried by the river is deposited in the reservoir basin, filling it in at a rapid rate. A small reservoir may fill in at a rate of 2 percent per year, meaning that sediment will fill the reservoir within 50 years.

Shown on these pages are the most common types of reservoirs found in North America.

Canyon reservoirs are deep, cold, clear and infertile. The main body is long and narrow and the creek arms may be half as long as the main lake. The shoreline slopes rapidly into depths that sometimes exceed 200 feet. Canyon reservoirs are best suited for rainbow trout, brown trout and lake trout, although some have decent largemouth bass and striper populations.

Highland and hill-land reservoirs are found in mountainous or hilly terrain. The main body of the reservoir is usually more than 100 feet deep, the shoreline slopes quite rapidly and the creek arms may be one-fourth as long as the main lake. These reservoirs support largemouth, smallmouth, white and striped bass, crappies and sunfish. A few have been stocked with muskies and some deeper ones hold trout.

Flatland reservoirs are located on flat or rolling terrain, so most of the basin is less than 50 feet deep. The main lake is wide and the creek arms, short. The fertile water supports largemouth and white bass, crappies, sunfish and catfish.

Prairie reservoirs may be more than 100 miles long and 100 feet deep, with short creek arms. The upper end is warm and shallow and has good numbers of walleyes and saugers. The lower end is cold and deep and may hold trout and salmon.

Desert reservoirs may be more than 100 feet deep, but they are usually located on fairly flat terrain, so the creek arms are short. Generally quite fertile, these lakes produce largemouth, smallmouth, white and striped bass, crappies and catfish.

MAN-MADE PONDS & PITS

Gravel pits and quarries vary greatly in size and depth. They have steep banks with no vegetation, so there is little gamefish cover. Adding brush piles often improves the fishing.

Farm ponds, also called "stock tanks" or just "tanks," are constructed for watering livestock, irrigating crops or controlling erosion. There are an estimated 3 million farm ponds in the United States, alone. Many of these ponds are stocked with fish, usually a combination of largemouth bass and bluegills, and provide excellent fishing.

Some ponds, however, are constructed for the sole purpose of sportfishing. Most of these are private, but there are many "fee-fishing" ponds where you pay by the pound or by the inch for what you

catch. These waters are usually well-stocked with catfish or trout.

Pits are nothing more than holes in the ground that fill with water after being mined or excavated for gravel, rock or fill.

Abandoned strip-mining pits are common in the East and Midwest. After filling, they are usually stocked with bass and bluegills, catfish or trout. New pits may be too acidic to support fish but, within a few years, the acidity starts to decline.

Gravel pits, borrow pits and rock quarries are found throughout the country. Their

Farm ponds are made by damming a creek or bulldozing or blasting a depression. Many ponds have to be sealed with a fine clay so they will hold water. Farm ponds usually measure from a fraction of an acre to 5 acres in surface area. In the North, ponds often need to be aerated to prevent winterkill.

water is usually quite clear and infertile, so they do not produce large fish crops. Some are cold enough to support trout, but most are stocked with bass and sunfish. Gravel pits and quarries are usually on private land, but borrow pits are along public highways. They remain after fill was removed for road construction.

Phosphate pits, most common in Florida, are extremely fertile. Many offer great fishing for trophy largemouths and also produce redear sunfish and catfish.

Iron-ore pits, found mainly in the Iron Range of northern Minnesota, have extremely cold, clear water that makes excellent habitat for rainbow and brown trout. Some shallow pits support bass, sunfish and crappies.

Phosphate pits range in size from 50 to more than 1,000 acres. They have irregular shorelines and are shallow and fertile, so they produce large crops of gamefish.

Iron-ore pits range from only a few acres to nearly 300 acres in surface area. Some are more than 500 feet deep. Because the water is so infertile, the depths remain well-oxygenated year-round.

Strip pits may be more than a mile in length, with depths exceeding 50 feet. The sides are usually quite steep and weedy or woody cover is minimal, so they may require extensive improvements in order to provide good fishing.

Borrow pits are generally shallower than gravel pits or rock quarries. Most have a rectangular shape, with straight shorelines, so the fish habitat they provide is less than ideal.

WARMWATER RIVERS & STREAMS

A mainstem river is the largest waterway in a given drainage system. It is fed by dozens or, sometimes, hundreds of smaller rivers which, in turn, are fed by numerous smaller streams and creeks. Many of these rivers have a network of dams that control flooding and keep water levels high enough for safe navigation. Most mainstem rivers have diverse habitat, including a system of backwaters, and an equally diverse fish population.

Warmwater rivers and streams are freshwater fishing's last frontier. Despite the abundance of flowing water in North America, more than 3 million miles in the United States alone, the vast majority of our fishing is done in lakes.

Every kind of warm- and coolwater gamefish can be found in warmwater rivers and streams. Just what fish species live in what streams depends mainly on current speed which, in turn, depends on the gradient, or slope, of the streambed.

In a low-gradient stream, the current speed is not fast enough to keep silt in suspension, so it settles out in the streambed, making for a mucky bottom that is best suited for largemouth bass, panfish and catfish. In a medium- to high-gradient stream, the current sweeps most of the silt away. The cleaner bottom is better for fish like smallmouth bass and walleyes.

Another important consideration is water clarity. If a stream is continually muddy, sight-feeding gamefish have a hard time finding food. Such streams are better suited for scent feeders, like catfish.

An irregular, winding streamcourse makes much better fish habitat than a straight

Southern bass rivers have slow-moving water and are often connected to swampy, cypress-studded backwaters. In addition to largemouth, they usually support crappies, sunfish and catfish.

Midwestern small-mouth streams have moderate current and a clean, rocky bottom that produces plenty of aquatic insects and crayfish. Besides smallmouth, these streams may support pike and walleye.

one. In a winding stream, the current excavates holes and undercuts along outside beds and deposits sediment on inside bends, creating sandbars. Such streams usually have an assortment of pools, riffles and runs.

Many streams have been intentionally straightened, or channelized. This allows water to pass through more quickly for purposes of flood control. These streams produce few gamefish.

Warmwater rivers and streams defy classification. There have been numerous attempts to devise a logical classification system but, with the staggering variety of moving water that exists, no one has come up with a useful method.

What fishermen are really interested in, however, is the quality of the fishery. On these pages are the types of rivers and streams that offer the best freshwater fishing.

Tidewater rivers are so named because their water levels are influenced by tides. The lower reaches are salty; the middle, brackish; and the upper, fresh. Many tidewater rivers have excellent fishing for largemouth and striped bass, and some have good runs of American shad.

Canadian pike rivers have slow to moderate current with a lot of weed growth. Pike abound in weedy areas; walleyes, in faster water. These rivers offer superb fishing, but access may be difficult.

TROUT STREAMS

Limestone streams are fed by springs with a high level of calcium carbonate. The nutrient-rich water has abundant weed growth and produces a good crop of insects and crustaceans, so trout are plentiful.

The term, "trout stream," refers to any stream that remains cold enough to support trout (or salmon) year-round. Almost any stream could support trout for nine or ten months out of the year, but only streams fed by groundwater sources or snowmelt at high elevations stay cold enough for trout during the hottest part of summer.

Although trout streams vary greatly in size, good streams have several characteristics (besides cold water) in common:
• A clean gravel or rubble bottom that produces an abundance of insect life.
• An irregular streambed consisting of riffles, pools and runs.
• A narrow, deep channel rather than a wide, shallow one that would expose too much water to the warming rays of the sun.
• A sufficient year-round flow, even under drought conditions.

• Enough shade along the banks to keep the water cool in summer.
• Relatively clear water.
• A medium gradient (opposite).

Most trout streams vary greatly over their length. Many are fed by a distinct source of cold water, such as a large spring, so they start out very cold and have a minimal flow. This type of habitat is best suited to brook trout, which thrive in the frigid water.

Farther downstream, tributaries flow in, increasing the flow and warming the water. The middle zone of the stream has the most insect life and often supports good numbers of brook, brown and rainbow trout.

As more and more tributaries enter the stream, its size increases even more and it gets warmer yet. The

Freestone streams are fed by runoff or infertile springs. Because of the low fertility, insect life is relatively scarce and plant growth, minimal. Unless there are fertile tributaries to add nutrients, trout populations are low to moderate.

streambed gradually flattens out and the bottom becomes siltier. Although the lower zone has the poorest habitat, it often yields the biggest trout. It's not unusual to catch a trophy brown in a big pool full of suckers and carp.

Many trout streams have been created by the construction of reservoirs. When water from the depths is discharged through a pipe at the base of the dam, the river below the dam may stay cold enough for trout for several miles.

Like warmwater rivers, trout streams are impossible to classify. But trout fishermen place them in two major categories, limestone and freestone, based on their fertility.

The Importance of Gradient

High-gradient streams have fast current with few pools or eddies to provide resting spots for trout. What fish there are will be found in stairstep-pools or behind boulders or log jams.

Low-gradient streams have a silty bottom that produces little insect life, and the water is usually too warm for trout. These streams may, however, produce a few large browns.

Medium-gradient streams have the riffle-run-pool habitat that trout prefer. The riffles make ideal feeding areas, and trout can rest in the deeper pools and runs. Medium-gradient streams also tend to meander, meaning that there are plenty of outside bends with deep holes and undercut banks.

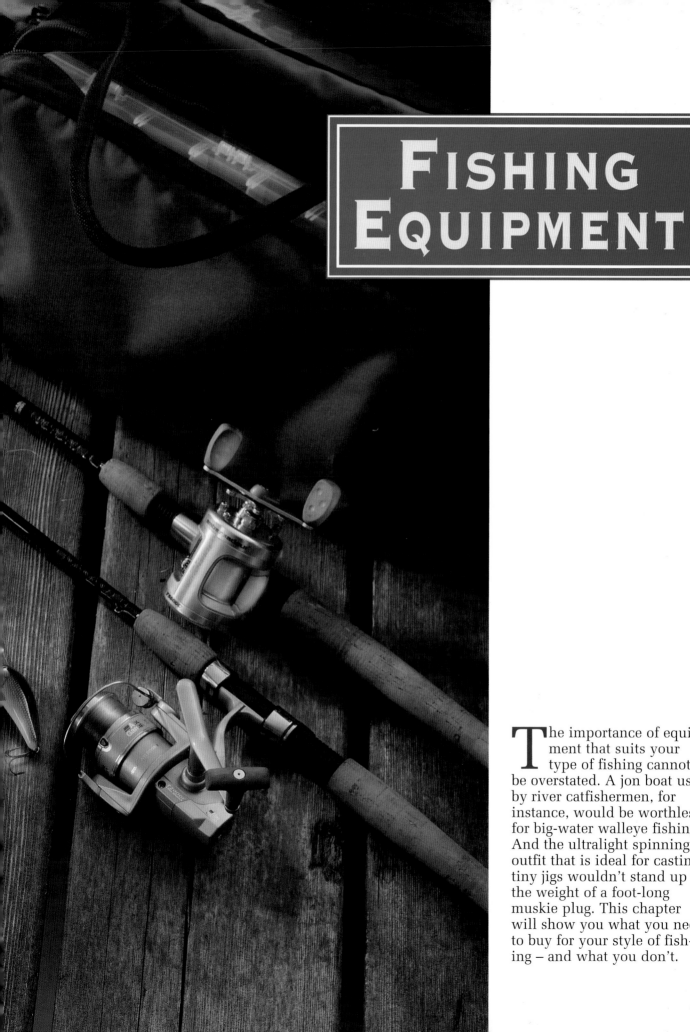

FISHING EQUIPMENT

The importance of equipment that suits your type of fishing cannot be overstated. A jon boat used by river catfishermen, for instance, would be worthless for big-water walleye fishing. And the ultralight spinning outfit that is ideal for casting tiny jigs wouldn't stand up to the weight of a foot-long muskie plug. This chapter will show you what you need to buy for your style of fishing – and what you don't.

FISHING RODS & REELS

Shopping for a fishing outfit at a well-stocked tackle shop can be a confusing experience. You'll see rods and reels of all sizes, colors and prices, with no explanation as to which rod goes with which reel or what outfit is intended for what purpose. Unless you're lucky enough to find a savvy sales clerk, you'll have to figure things out for yourself.

Your selection depends on a combination of factors: the size of the fish you expect to catch, the size of the baits you'll be using and the type of cover in which you'll be fishing.

With a light spinning outfit and 6-pound line, you could land a 20-pound pike in unobstructed water. But you wouldn't be able to toss a heavy lure with such a light outfit and, in heavy weeds,

Baitcasting gear enables you to cast very accurately. By thumbing the spool, you can stop the lure right on your target. The relatively stiff rod and sturdy reel with a rotating spool easily handles heavy line, so you can cast heavy lures and extract good-sized fish from dense cover. The biggest drawback to baitcasting gear is the backlashing problem, but with a little practice, it won't be a major concern.

the fish would make short work of the light line. You'd be better advised to use a sturdy baitcasting outfit with 20-pound line.

If you do many different kinds of fishing, you'll probably need several different outfits. These pages will explain what gear is best for your style of fishing.

Spinning gear is the best choice for casting light lures. It also excels for distance casting because line flows easily off the open-face reel. When you flip the bail, the line comes off the end of the spool in loose coils, so the rod must have large guides to reduce line friction. Because there is no rotating spool, spinning gear cannot backlash, but twisted line can still cause nasty snarls.

Flycasting gear is needed to cast heavy fly line, which, in turn, propels the nearly weightless fly. Picking up and casting heavy line requires a long rod, usually from 8 to 9 feet in length. A long rod also helps in controlling the line and playing fish. Fly rods carry a weight designation, usually from 3- to 10-weight, that matches the weight of the line they're designed to cast.

Trolling outfits have the large-capacity reels needed for long-line trolling or downrigger fishing. The reels are not designed for casting. Trolling rods may be short and stiff for trolling heavy baits, or long and flexible for downrigger fishing. Although sensitivity is not an issue, many anglers prefer graphite trolling rods because they telegraph the action of the lure better than fiberglass.

Selecting Rods

You may be shocked at the price of today's top-shelf fishing rods, but you don't need to spend a fortune to get a rod that will catch just as many fish as the high-buck models.

When selecting a rod, here's what you really need to consider:

• **Length -** A long rod gives you better casting distance and accuracy, and allows you to cast lighter baits. It also gives you better line control and more powerful hooksets.

But a short rod enables you to set the hook more quickly and works better for casting in close quarters.

• **Action -** Slow-action rods work best for casting light baits. They're a good choice for live-bait fishing, because fish feel little resistance when they swim off with the bait. Slow-action rods also help in fighting fish, because the rod bends instead of the line breaking. Fast-action rods give you better sensitivity and a quicker hookset.

• **Power -** Just how much power you need in a rod depends on the weight of your lure or bait, the size of fish and the thickness of the cover. The difference between the terms, "power" and "action," is illustrated below.

• **Modulus -** The strength of the rod material is measured in modulus. In general, the higher the modulus, the lighter and more sensitive the rod, but the more brittle it will be.

Action vs. Power

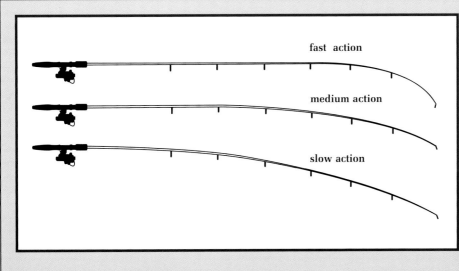

The term "action" is defined as where the rod flexes. A fast-action rod flexes mainly near the tip; a medium action starts flexing in the middle; a slow-action flexes over its entire length. The problem is, when sales clerks refer to a "medium-action" rod, they usually mean medium-power.

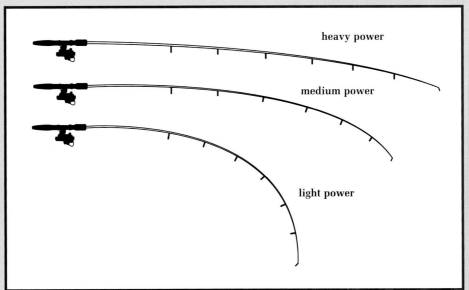

The term "power" refers to the rod's stiffness. It takes much more force to bend a heavy-power rod than it does a light-power. This illustration shows how much bend a given weight puts in heavy-, medium- and light-power spinning rods.

Selecting Reels

Too many anglers spend a lot of money on a fishing rod and then pair it with a cheap reel. That's not a wise decision.

On the surface, an inexpensive reel may look pretty much like a pricey one, but the differences will be apparent when you start fishing. Cheap reels have fewer ball bearings in the drive mechanism, so they aren't nearly as smooth. They are usually heavier, and they often have sticky drags. Some even have gears made of a low-grade metal that will stand little abuse.

In the case of fly fishing reels, however, quality is much less important, because the reel has no function in casting; it merely serves to store the fly line. But how fast you can take up line depends on whether you buy a single-action, whose spool turns one time for each turn of the reel handle, or a multiplier, whose spool turns more than once.

The reel you select must balance with the rod. If the reel is too heavy, the rod will feel butt-heavy, making the tip seem less sensitive. If the reel is too light, the rod will feel tip-heavy, and keeping the tip up will tire your wrist. Before buying a rod and reel, hold it in your hand to make sure it is well balanced.

On this page are a few tips for selecting spinning, baitcasting and trolling reels.

For better casting performance, select a spinning reel with a long, wide spool, rather than a short, narrow one. A long spool holds more line, so the line won't slap against the spool rim toward the end of the cast. A wide spool minimizes line kinking.

A front drag on a spinning reel is generally smoother than a rear drag. A front drag has large washers that exert pressure on a flat surface. A rear drag pushes against the drive shaft, which has a much smaller surface area.

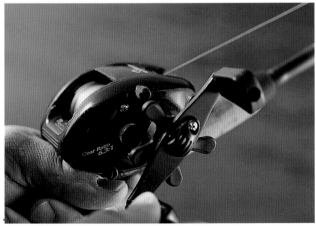

Use a high-speed reel (gear-ratio of at least 6:1) when you need a fast retrieve, or to pick up line in a hurry. A high-speed reel is a must for long-line trolling, where you may have to reel in 200 feet of line.

A trolling reel with a line counter makes it easy to reset your line at the same distance after catching a fish. Without a counter, you would have to count the passes of the level-wind bar or somehow mark the line.

FISHING LINE

When "superlines" were first introduced in the early 1990s, many folks assumed that they would soon dominate the fishing-line market. These super-thin lines, made of the same space-age materials used to make bullet-proof vests, had virtually no stretch, so they provided excellent sensitivity and powerful hooksets.

But superlines have not revolutionized the sport. They certainly have their place, but the vast majority of anglers still rely on monofilament for most of their fishing. The fact remains that mono is nearly invisible in water, which is a major advantage when dealing with finicky biters. And the stretch factor that everyone complained about turns out not to be so bad after all. It provides an extra cushion in fighting fish, and your rod won't snap on the hookset, as it sometimes does with superlines.

The information on these pages will help you select the right line for the type of fishing you do.

When selecting monofilament line, the main considerations are limpness, stretch and color. A very limp line, such as Trilene XL (extra limp), works well for casting, because the line doesn't form stiff coils that rub on the guides. A line with a harder finish, like Trilene XT (extra tough), is a better choice when fishing in weeds or rocks that could cause scuffing. Most experienced anglers use clear or green mono when fishing in clear water. Fluorescent line is easy to see and is a good choice in discolored water.

Superlines, usually made of Spectra, are about four times as strong as monofilament of the same diameter. They work exceptionally well for deep-water jigging or trolling. Mono has too much stretch for solid hooksets in deep water, and it is difficult to get down while trolling because its large diameter creates so much water resistance.

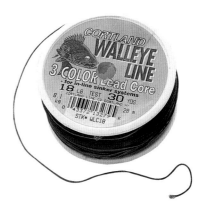

Lead-core line is used for deep trolling. It is color-coded, so when you start catching fish at a certain depth, you can easily return to that depth by letting the line out to the same color.

Weight-forward

Double-taper

Shooting-taper

Level

Fly lines come in a variety of tapers for different fishing purposes. Weight-forward (WF) lines have a thick belly behind the front taper, so they cast easily. Double-taper (DT) lines land delicately; they taper at both ends, so when one end wears out, you can reverse the line. Shooting-taper (ST) lines, also called shooting-head lines, give you maximum casting distance; they have a heavy front end and a long monofilament "running line." Level (L) lines have an equal diameter over their length. Though inexpensive, they are difficult to cast, so few anglers now use them. Be sure to match the weight of your fly line to your fly rod (p.33).

Braided Dacron is used mainly on heavy baitcasting outfits, usually for pike or muskie fishing. It is also a popular choice for backing on a fly reel.

Sinking

Floating

Sink-tip

Wire line is often used for deep trolling and jigging. There are two types: braided and single-strand. The latter is thinner, but kinks much easier. Wire is losing popularity because of superlines.

Fly lines are designated as floating (F), used mainly for dry-fly fishing; floating/sinking (F/S), also called sink-tip, for moderately deep presentations; and sinking (S), for deep presentations.

TOOLS & ACCESSORIES

A well-equipped angler probably has two or three tackle boxes and a half-dozen rods in the boat, but may not remember some of the little things that are sometimes needed on a fishing trip.

Besides the items shown on these pages, here is a list of things that you'll probably want to keep in your boat:

• A tool kit, including extra boat fuses and wire connectors.

• A first-aid kit, for tending to fish cuts and other injuries.

• Matches, in case you need to start a fire for shore lunch or to warm up in chilly weather.

• A flashlight, in case you are stuck on the water after dark.

• A camera, for proving you caught what you claim to have released.

• A fire extinguisher, now a requirement in many states.

• Sunscreen.

• Life jackets and other required safety equipment.

• Rain gear.

A marine-band radio is highly recommended if you fish big water. Not only does it have a weather band to inform you of approaching storms, you can use it to trade fishing information with friends.

A long-handled hook remover or a hemostat helps safely remove hooks from deep in a fish's mouth. If you try to use an ordinary pliers to remove hooks, you may injure the fish.

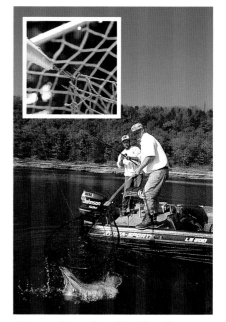

Carry a long-handled landing net so you can reach fish that don't want to come close to the boat. Don't use a net with a loose weave; your hooks will constantly catch in the braid.

An accessory rack provides handy storage for items such as a hook remover, hook file, nail clippers and pliers. With an accessory rack, you'll always know where to find your tools.

A plug "knocker" comes in handy if you do a lot of fishing in snaggy areas. This model clips onto your line and slides down on a string to jar your bait loose.

Carry an accurate scale so you can get the exact weight of fish you want to release.

Soft-packs make the ideal tackle-storage system, because they have pockets for gear of a variety of sizes. You can store different types of baits in individual plastic boxes, and take along only the boxes you need for a day's fishing.

An electric thermometer is a big help in locating the thermocline, finding spring holes or detecting other water temperature changes that could help you locate fish.

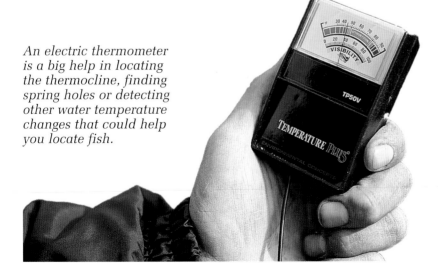

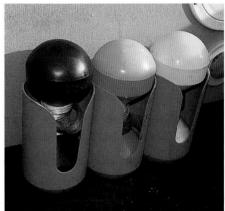

Marker buoys are a must for pinpointing precise spots on deep structure. This rack provides storage for three marker buoys.

MODERN TROLLING GEAR

Trolling is one of the oldest fishing methods, but new innovations in equipment have made the technique more effective than ever.

In the old days, there was a lot of guesswork involved in trolling. You were never sure how deep your lure was running or what depth the fish were at. All you could do was experiment until you found them.

Today, you can use sophisticated electronics to pinpoint the depth of fish, and then set downriggers to present your lures at precisely the right level.

If you really want to go high-tech, you can buy a unit that gives you water temperature and trolling speed at the downrigger, so you know you're trolling in the right temperature zone and moving at the right speed.

You can also buy bottom-tracking downriggers that have a built-in sonar to keep the cannonball at a pre-set distance off the bottom. When the water gets shallower, the cannonball automatically comes up; when it gets deeper, it goes down.

Downriggers enable you to cover water vertically but, to cover it horizontally, you'll need side planers. By fishing downriggers and side planers together, you could cover a swath of water more than 100 feet wide and 100 feet deep.

On these pages are the most important types of gear used by modern-day trollers.

Understanding Downriggers

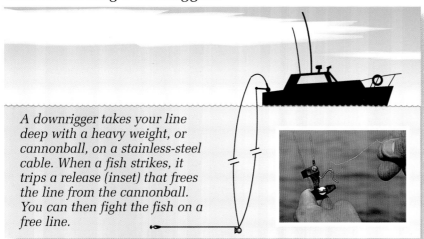

A downrigger takes your line deep with a heavy weight, or cannonball, on a stainless-steel cable. When a fish strikes, it trips a release (inset) that frees the line from the cannonball. You can then fight the fish on a free line.

Other Trolling Equipment

Side planers attach to the line, pulling it to the side. They can be rigged two ways. (1) When a fish strikes, the planer detaches from the line; you land the fish and go back to pick up the planer. (2) The planer stays on the line and you reel it in with the fish.

A diving planer takes your line down and to the side. In order for the planer to dive, the bar (arrow) must be locked in the groove. When a fish strikes, the bar breaks free, causing the planer to flatten out so you can easily reel it in, along with the fish.

A speed indicator keeps your lures moving at precisely the right speed, despite wind or current. This model monitors current speed and water temperature, both at the surface and at downrigger level.

Trolling boards are attached by a cord to an elevated mast. The fishing line is attached to a release (inset) which slides down the cord until you lock the reel to stop it. When a fish strikes, it trips the release, allowing you to fight the fish on a free line. With boards out both sides of the boat, you can cover a swath more than 100 feet wide.

Rod holders pointing out to the side, as shown, help trollers cover more water. Some anglers use rods up to 9 feet long; this way, they can spread their lures about 25 feet without using planers.

ICE FISHING GEAR

Modern technology has had a major impact on every aspect of freshwater fishing, and ice fishing is no exception. Changes in the sport over the past decade have been enormous.

No longer do savvy ice fishermen spend all day sitting in a shanty, watching their line in hopes that a fish will happen along.

Today, they find a productive spot, possibly using a handheld GPS to return to a waypoint that produced during the open-water season. Then, they drill a couple dozen holes with a super-sharp auger. Using a portable shelter, they fish each hole for a few minutes while looking for fish on their flasher. If nothing shows up, they're off to try another waypoint.

Mobility is the name of the game in modern ice fishing. You've got to keep moving to find the fish, just as you would in summer. The equipment on these pages makes mobility a lot easier.

Rig your flasher on a "blue box" for portability. A motorcycle or gel-cel battery provides enough power for two or three days of fishing. The transducer can be set on a rigid rod (above), or you can use a self-leveling transducer.

Things to Look For in an Ice Fishing Flasher

A self-leveling transducer enables you to move from hole to hole without stopping to level the transducer after each move.

A backlit screen is much easier to see at night. With a regular screen, you can see the signal, but not the numbers on the dial.

For fishing in water more than 50 feet deep, use a unit with at least 1,000 watts of peak-to-peak power.

Other Important Ice-Fishing Equipment

Tip-ups make it possible to spread out your lines and cover more water. They have an underwater reel and a flag that pops up when a fish bites.

A graphite jigging rod gives you the sensitivity you need to detect subtle wintertime bites. Select one with the right power for your type of fishing.

Portable shelters make it easy to move from spot to spot. This model has a flip-up top and doubles as a sled that can tow your gear.

Ice cleats attach to the bottom of your boots to give you traction on slippery ice. Cleats are usually not necessary when there is snow on the ice.

A flashlight-type depth finder lets you easily check the depth before drilling your holes. Just set it in a little water, and it will sound through the ice.

Use a fast-cutting auger so you can drill plenty of holes. Most modern augers will cut through a foot of ice in five seconds or less.

Specially designed sleds have a place to carry your auger, minnow bucket, depth finder, rods, tip-ups and other accessories, such as an ice scoop, lure box and chisel (for testing ice thickness).

FISHING BOATS

Bass boats are designed for speed and fishing ease. The low-profile fiberglass or aluminum hull enables anglers to fish shallow water, and the elevated bow and stern decks make casting easy. Bass boats range from 17 to 21 feet in length and are powered by 75- to 225-horsepower outboards. Some can reach speeds exceeding 70 miles per hour.

There is no single boat suited to all types of fishing. Many would argue that a well-equipped bass boat is the ultimate fishing machine, but you wouldn't be able to use it in waters that don't have a good boat ramp, and it wouldn't handle big water as well as a walleye boat. Don't buy a boat because of its

Aluminum semi-Vs are the perfect all-purpose fishing boats. They're very light, yet can handle fairly rough water. Most are 14 to 18 feet long and designed for tiller-operated outboards, usually 25 to 50 hp. Small semi-Vs usually have bench seats; larger ones, pedestal seats.

flashy looks; be sure it suits your style of fishing and the waters you fish.

One of the biggest decisions in buying a boat is choosing the hull material. Fiberglass hulls can be molded in such a way that they easily part the waves, making for a smooth ride. Many have beautiful metal-flake finishes. Aluminum hulls are lighter, more durable and less expensive.

Shown here are some of the most popular types of boats used in freshwater angling.

Walleye boats are designed for big water. They have a deep-V aluminum or fiberglass hull that can handle big waves. They come in tiller and console models from 16 to 19 feet in length and are powered by 50- to 225-horsepower motors.

Canoes are a good choice for fishing hard-to-reach waters. They're easy to portage and paddle, but are quite unstable. Some models have a square stern that accommodates a small outboard. Or, you can rig a regular canoe with a motor bracket.

Jon boats, because of their flat bottom, are very stable and ideal for use in shallow water. Models with a square bow, however, are not a good choice in rough water. Some have a semi-V bow (shown), which helps split the waves.

OUTBOARD MOTORS

When selecting an outboard, remember that a little extra power often comes in handy. If your boat is rated for 60 horsepower, for example, you could probably get by with 50 horsepower, but it may be hard to get up on plane with a full load of anglers and gear. The extra power also helps control your boat in rough water and gets you in faster when a storm threatens. A bigger motor may even give you better fuel economy, because your boat is on plane rather than plowing water.

For many anglers, trolling speed is an important issue. Before buying a particular

outboard, ask a fisherman who has one how it trolls.

Another important consideration is the type of propeller. You can get by with an aluminum prop, but a stainless-steel prop will improve performance and take a lot more abuse. Although stainless-steel props are considerably more expensive than aluminum, they will probably save you money in the long run.

Be sure your propeller has the right pitch for your boat. You'll normally find a number designating the pitch stamped somewhere on the propeller. A 13-pitch prop, for instance, pushes the boat forward 13

inches with each turn. You may have to try several different props to find the one that gives you the right combination of speed and power.

Until recently, practically all outboards were 2-cycle, meaning you had to mix oil with the gas. But when studies began to show that exhaust from 2-cycle motors was polluting the water, some manufacturers began making 4-cycle outboards.

Although 4-cycles are bigger and more expensive, they run quieter and smoother and burn much less gas. Many anglers who have made the switch say they'll never go back to a 2-cycle.

"Kicker" motors are small outboards used on large fishing boats for trolling or as an emergency backup should the main outboard fail. Kickers range in size from 2 to 15 horsepower.

Electric Trolling Motors

For precise boat control, an electric trolling motor is a must. Not only is an electric much quieter than an outboard, you don't have to spend the day inhaling gas fumes.

A bow-mount trolling motor with a foot control is the best choice for casting, because it leaves your hands free. But for trolling, many anglers prefer a transom-mount. By backtrolling (trolling in reverse), you can follow a specific contour much more closely, because the transom is not blown off course by the wind as much as the bow.

It pays to select a motor with more power than you think is necessary. Then, you can make quick course corrections to stay on fish.

Many boats are rigged with a pair of trolling motors. The bow-mount is used for casting and the transom-mount for backtrolling.

Handy Trolling Motor Features

A bow mount with a foot control frees your hands for casting. Some models have electronic foot controls, so there is no clumsy cable.

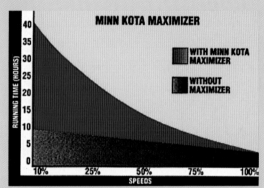

A Maximizer is an electronic device that makes your trolling motor more efficient. As this graph shows, your battery will last twice as long with a Maximizer at 50% speed; 4 times as long at 10%.

An extension handle makes steering easier. Instead of stretching your arm and contorting your body to reach the handle, you can steer comfortably from your seat.

A reversible head enables you to backtroll with much more power. By spinning the head 180 degrees on the shaft and reattaching it, you can backtroll in forward rather than reverse.

FISHING BOAT OPTIONS

Most of today's fishing boats come well-equipped, but it pays to do a little shopping to make sure you're getting the right options for the type of fishing you do.

One thing you can never have enough of is storage space, particularly dry storage. Look for a boat that has compartments with sealed lids, otherwise your gear will mildew.

With all the electronic gear found on modern fishing boats, you'll need enough space to store two, maybe three batteries. Besides a starting battery, you'll need one or two others to power your trolling motor. Don't attempt to use

An electronics compartment protects your depth finder, GPS, marine radio, etc., from rain and boat spray. The compartment should be lockable and large enough to house all your electronic gear.

Hydraulic seats smooth out the ride in rough water. A lever on the pedestal allows you to raise or lower the seat. Many anglers install extra bases, so the seats can be rearranged as needed.

the same battery for both purposes or you may wind up paddling home.

You certainly don't need a stereo system with a tape deck in order to catch fish, but a radio with a weather band serves an important safety function.

Here are some of the most important fishing boat options.

A rod locker should be at least 7 feet long and large enough to hold a half-dozen rods. If the locker is too short or too small, you'll damage your rods when removing them or putting them away.

An aerated livewell is a must for anyone who needs to keep their fish in good condition. Some livewells are equipped with a timer, so they run intermittently and save battery power.

Splash guards make it possible to backtroll in rough water without waves splashing over your head. The best splash guards are made of indestructible Lexan and attach with thumb screws.

A bilge pump enables you to easily drain water from a heavy rain or from trolling in big waves. Some bilge pumps are automatic, turning on whenever the water reaches a certain level.

An on-board charging system makes battery charging a snap. All you have to do is plug the charger into an extension cord, and it will charge all of the boat's batteries.

Storage compartments should be large enough to hold items like tackle boxes and tool kits. Dry storage is a must for rain gear, life preservers, extra jackets or anything that could mildew.

BOAT TRAILERS

When shopping for a fishing rig, most anglers put a great deal of thought into choosing the right boat and motor, but the trailer is of much less concern.

If you wind up with the wrong trailer, however, you'll have trouble launching and loading your boat, and your hull could suffer serious damage.

The most common mistake is selecting a trailer that is too light for your boat. Be sure the trailer you select is rated for several hundred pounds more than the combined weight of the boat, motor and gear you'll be carrying. Otherwise, the frame may buckle or the axle bend when you hit a bump.

If you choose a roller trailer, be sure there are enough rollers to distribute the boat's weight. With only a few rollers, a bumpy road could crack the hull.

On these pages are some tips for selecting the right trailer and outfitting it with the right equipment. We'll also show you how to "power-load" your boat.

Roller trailers work well with aluminum boats. The best trailers have a set of rollers in both the front and back. If the rollers are adjusted properly, the boat will center itself when you drive it on (opposite).

Bunk trailers are the best choice for fiberglass boats, because they give the hull full-length support. With rollers, too much pressure is exerted on a small area of the hull, sometimes causing cracks.

How to Power-Load with a Drive-On Trailer

1 Back the trailer in just far enough that the rear rollers or bunks are at water level. If you back in too far, the rollers or bunks will be too deep to center the boat.

2 Trim up your outboard at least one-third of the way to prevent the prop from hitting bottom when you drive on.

3 Line the boat up so it is centered in the rear roller and then run the boat forward until it just bumps the roller on the winch stand.

4 Hook up the winch rope and safety chain, tilt up your motor and drive the boat out. With a little practice, you can load in less than a minute.

Handy Boat Trailer Features

A tongue jack comes in handy for lifting the trailer to hook it up or unhook it from your vehicle.

Bearing Buddies have zerts that make it easy to add grease to your wheel bearings.

A spare-tire carrier bolts to your boat trailer, so you don't have to carry the spare in your vehicle.

DEPTH FINDERS

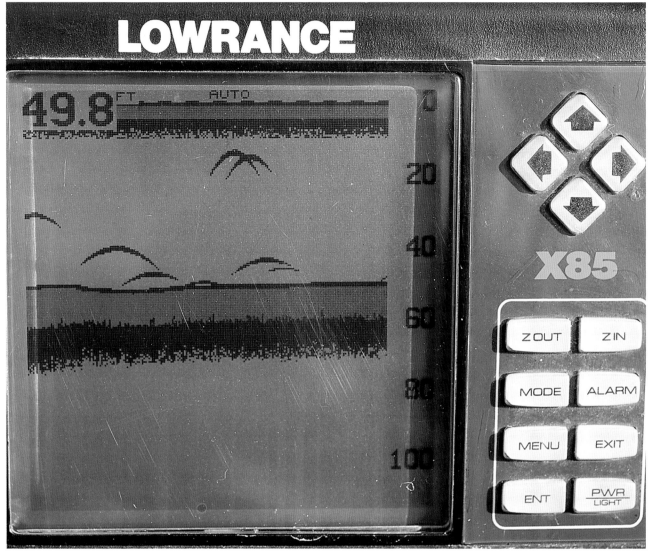

Liquid-crystal recorders (LCRs) are, by far, the most popular type of depth finder. They have a display consisting of tiny "pixels." The smaller the pixels, the better the resolution. A good unit generally has a vertical pixel count of at least 160, and the best units have more than 200. Liquid-crystals are not recommended at temperatures below 20°F, however, because the signal is slow to appear on the screen.

Ask a veteran angler to name his or her most important piece of equipment, and the answer will most likely be a depth finder. A good depth finder gives fishermen "underwater eyes," making it possible to find the right structure and even see the fish.

All depth finders operate the same way: a transducer sends a sonar signal to the bottom and picks up the returning echo. The time differential determines the depth. If the signal hits fish or weeds, their depth will be recorded as well.

The main difference between the various types of depth finders is in the way the reading is displayed. A flasher, for instance, gives you exactly the same information as a liquid-crystal, but the reading appears on a dial, rather than a screen.

One of the most important considerations in choosing a depth finder is the transducer's cone angle. The higher the transducer's frequency, the narrower the cone of sound that it emits. A narrow cone (20 degrees or less) is best for detecting fish lying close to the bottom. A wider cone is a better choice when you want to see more of the bottom or watch your lure, as you may wish to do while vertically jigging.

Although the types of depth finders shown on these pages make up the vast majority of the market, some anglers still prefer paper graphs, because they provide a permanent record. Should you turn away from the dial for a few seconds, you could miss seeing a fish on a liq-

uid-crystal, but it will still be there on a paper graph.

Whatever type of depth finder you buy, you must learn to adjust it properly and interpret its signals. That information is presented on pp.68-69.

Other Popular Depth Finders

Liquid-crystal flashers display the signal on a round dial, rather than a rectangular screen. Compared to color flashers, these units are easier to read on a sunny day, and they have a backlit dial for night fishing.

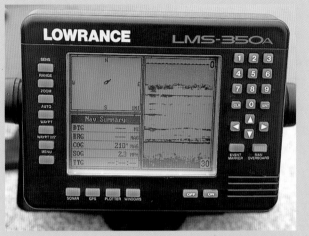

Combination units can be switched from an LCR to a GPS by pushing a button. If desired, you can split the screen to get sonar and navigation information at the same time.

Color flashers are very sensitive and display signals in different colors, depending on target size and position in the cone. But they are hard to read in direct sun and may not have enough power for use in very deep water.

Color videos provide the best resolution of any depth finder. The signal is displayed on a cathode-ray tube (CRT) like that of a TV set, with different size targets shown in different colors. On the downside, videos are bulky and hard to read in direct sun.

NAVIGATION DEVICES

Not long ago, fishermen were marveling at the magic of Loran (long-range navigation) devices. Finally, anglers on big lakes could return unerringly to a precise spot where they had caught fish in the past.

But the popularity of Loran has been limited by several factors: it depends on signals from Coast Guard towers, so it doesn't work everywhere, many anglers find it difficult to use and it can be affected by storms. It also requires a long whip antenna to pick up the signals and it processes them very slowly.

GPS (Global Positioning System) technology has greatly simplified the navigation process. It is the same technology the U.S. armed forces uses to guide their "smart bombs."

But concerns that GPS technology could fall into the wrong hands have led the U.S. government to downgrade the GPS signal available to the public. With a clean signal, GPS could put you within a few feet of your spot; with the downgraded signal, 50 to 200 feet. There have been rumors that the government will soon be offering a clean signal, but at this printing, it is still being downgraded.

For specifics on how to use GPS navigators, turn to pages 70-71.

Handheld GPS units are rapidly gaining popularity because of their portability and low cost. But the small screen can be difficult to read, especially in plotter mode (opposite).

Important GPS Features

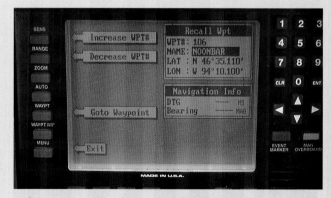

Be sure the GPS unit you buy has a parallel channel receiver. By processing signals from different satellites at the same time, rather than separately, the unit responds more quickly and has better accuracy.

Select a unit that has enough memory to store all the waypoints (destinations) that you want to save. For most anglers, 200 waypoints is plenty, but those who fish many different waters may need a lot more.

GPS units are much more reliable than Loran units. They work anywhere in the world and are not affected by weather. They have a module that picks up signals from at least four satellites, and the data is processed in seconds, so you can navigate much more accurately.

Make sure the unit has a plotter screen with a minimum scale of no more than .1 miles. This way, you will be able to closely track the boat's path in relation to a waypoint. With a larger minimum scale, it would be difficult to tell.

A steering screen is a handy feature because it allows you to navigate to your waypoint simply by keeping the boat icon on the center line until it arrives at the waypoint.

FISHING SKILLS

Owning all the right equipment is one matter; learning to use it properly is another. It does you little good to own an expensive rod and reel, for instance, if you can't put your bait anywhere near your target.

In this chapter, we'll give you some pointers on basic skills like casting, tying knots and reading hydrographic maps. We'll also give you a quick course on using electronics. Then, we'll help you master one of the toughest skills of all: boat control.

CASTING

A beginning angler just learning to cast wants to throw the bait halfway across the county. An experienced angler practices tossing the bait into a coffee cup only a few feet away. You soon learn that accuracy is a lot more important than distance in most types of fishing. Nevertheless, you should know how to make a long cast when the situation requires it.

The biggest mistake of most novice casters is trying to throw the bait rather than cast it. They whip the rod as hard as they can, and the bait flies erratically, usually not too far. A veteran caster, on the other hand, lets the rod do the work. Snapping the rod back with a flick of the wrist lets the natural spring of the rod propel the bait.

For good casting performance, you need a rod that suits the weight of the bait you're using. If you try to cast a light lure with a stiff rod, it won't flex, or *load*, enough on the backcast, so there won't be enough forward spring. If you try to cast a heavy lure with a whippy rod, it will flex too much and won't have enough power to recover.

The rod's action (where it bends) is also important. A slow action works best for very light baits, because the entire rod flexes to generate more tip speed. Length is also important. A long rod is the best choice for distance casting, because it has more leverage. But a short rod is better for flicking the bait under a bush.

Casting with a Baitcasting Outfit

Adjust your spool tension so the weight of the lure slowly pulls line off the spool.

With the reel in free spool and about a foot of line hanging off the rod, firmly thumb the spool to prevent it from turning.

Briskly draw the rod into the backcast and stop it at about 2 o'clock. For accuracy, bring it straight back over your shoulder.

Cast with a smooth forward stroke, releasing your thumb from the spool when the rod is at about 10 o'clock.

Prevent backlashes by lightly thumbing the spool as necessary as the line flows out. Thumb the spool harder to stop the lure on a precise spot.

Be sure to choose a rod with closely spaced guides. Otherwise, the line will form a belly between the guides and slap against the rod, shortening your casts. The guides should be large enough that they don't restrict the flow of line off the reel (p.61).

A spinning reel with a long, wide spool will cast farther than one with a short, narrow spool. A wide-spool baitcasting reel will also cast farther than one with a narrow spool, but the latter is not as likely to backlash.

The spool should be filled almost, but not quite, to the lip. If the line level is too low, the line will slap against the lip and your casts will fall short. If you overfill the spool, the line will spring off and cause tangles.

Strive for accuracy, not distance.

Casting with a Spinning Outfit

Fill the reel to within about ¹/₈ inch of the lip of the spool. If the line level is low, line will slap the edge of spool when you cast.

Open the bail and pick up the line with your index finger. Leave about a foot of line hanging off the end of the rod.

Briskly draw the rod into the backcast and stop it at about 2 o'clock. The lure's weight should put a sharp bend in the rod.

Cast with a smooth forward stroke, releasing the line from your index finger when the rod is at about 10 o'clock.

Control casting distance by brushing the line with your index finger as it flows off the spool.

1 Strip off line as much line as you think you'll need. Let it pile neatly at your feet or float downstream with the current. Then, point your rod in the direction you wish to cast, lift the rod and smoothly accelerate until all of the line is in the air.

2 Propel the line into the backcast with a short, fast "speed stroke." This causes the rod to bend and generates enough power to draw the line backward.

3 Stop the rod just past the vertical and allow a loop to form as the line shoots backward.

4 Wait until the backcast unrolls into a narrow, J-shaped loop.

5 Sharply stroke the rod forward and then stop it abruptly at the position shown. The line should shoot forward and settle gently to the water. Lower the rod tip to begin fishing.

After making a long cast, place a piece of electrical tape on the spool of your baitcaster. Then, should you get a backlash, the tangle can't go any deeper than the tape.

Long-handled rods give you extra casting distance. Not only does the extra length provide more leverage, you can grip the handle with both hands to generate more power.

Use a baitcasting reel with a narrow spool for short-range casting. Because the spool is lighter than a wider spool, it has considerably less momentum, so it is less likely to backlash.

A short rod is the best choice for casting in tight spots. When you're fishing in a narrow, brushy stream, for example, you don't have enough room for a casting stroke with a long rod.

Use a spinning rod with guides that are large enough so the line coils don't rub on them when you cast. The friction will reduce casting distance.

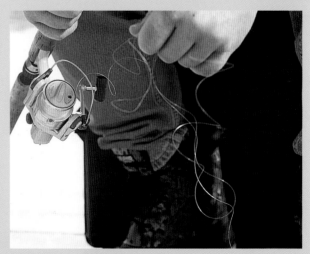

Discard any old, kinky monofilament. Not only is kinky line hard to cast, it is usually much weaker than fresh mono.

TYING KNOTS

Learning to tie good knots is one of the most important fishing skills. Even a strong, well-tied knot may be the weakest link between you and the fish, and a poorly tied knot practically guarantees losing any big fish that you hook.

The more kinds of fishing you do, the more knots you'll need to learn. Fly fishermen, for instance, use different knots than spin fishermen. Saltwater anglers use still different knots. And some of the knots that work well with mono are a poor choice with superlines.

Dozens of different knots have been devised for different fishing purposes. But some of them are so difficult to tie that you'd need an instruction manual in the boat. The best advice is to learn a few easy-to-tie knots and practice until you have them down pat.

Whatever knot you tie, it's a good practice to moisten it before snugging it up. This reduces abrasion that could weaken the line. After the knot is snugged up, test it by giving it a firm tug; better to break then than after you hook a fish.

Retie your knots periodically throughout the day. Repeated casting weakens knots, as does catching fish. When you retie, strip off a few feet of line ahead of the knot to get rid of any abraded spots.

Shown on these pages are some of the most useful fishing knots.

Attaching Line to Spool—Arbor Knot

The arbor knot is so named because it tightens firmly around the arbor, preventing the line from slipping when you reel.

(1) Pass the line around the spool, *(2)* wrap the free end around the standing line and make an overhand knot, *(3)* make an overhand knot in the free end, *(4)* snug up the knot by pulling on the standing line; the knot should tighten firmly around the arbor.

Attaching Hook or Lure—Trilene Knot

The Trilene knot has a double loop around the hook eye and is one of the strongest hook-attachment knots.

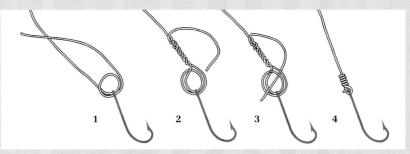

(1) Form a double loop by passing the free end through the hook eye twice, *(2)* wrap the free end around the standing line 4-5 times, *(3)* pass the free end through the double loop, *(4)* pull on the standing line and hook to snug up the knot.

Attaching Hook or Lure—Palomar Knot

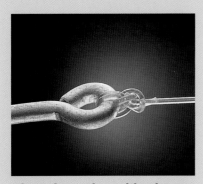

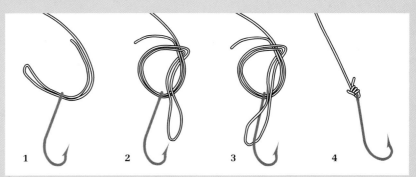

The Palomar knot, like the Trilene knot, has a double loop around the hook eye. But some anglers find it easier to tie.

(1) Form a double line then push it through the hook eye; (2) with the double line, make an overhand knot around the standing line and free end; (3) put the hook through the loop; (4) hold the hook while pulling on the standing line and free end to snug up the knot.

Attaching Hook or Lure—Loop Knot

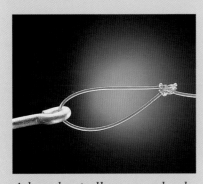

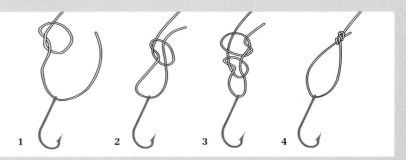

A loop knot allows your hook or lure to swing more freely, so it has better action than a hook or lure that is snubbed down tightly.

(1) Make an overhand knot several inches from the end of the line and put the free end through the hook eye; (2) pass the free end through the overhand knot; (3) with the free end, make an overhand knot around the standing line (where you tie the second overhand determines the size of the loop); (4) tighten the overhand knots and pull the standing line to snug up the knot.

Tying a Loop—Double Surgeon's Loop

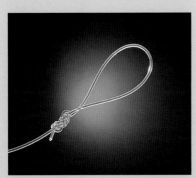

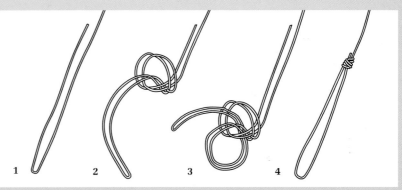

The double surgeon's loop is very easy to tie and makes a secure loop in the end of your line or leader.

(1) Form a double line, (2) tie an overhand knot in it, (3) pass the doubled line through the overhand knot again, (4) pull on the loop and standing line to snug up the knot.

Splicing Lines—Bloodknot

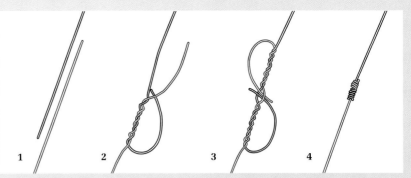

A blood knot looks complex, but is quite simple to tie. Don't try it with lines of greatly different diameters or different materials.

(1) Hold the lines alongside each other, with the ends facing opposite directions; *(2)* wrap one line around the other 4-5 times, and pass the free end between the two lines, as shown; *(3)* repeat step 2 with the other line; *(4)* pull on both lines to snug up the knot.

Splicing Lines—Double Uni-Knot

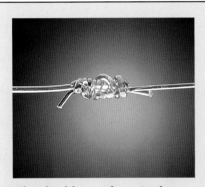

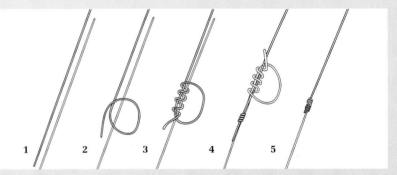

The double uni-knot is the best way to splice mono to superline. It works well for any lines of different material or diameter.

(1) Hold the lines alongside each other, with the ends facing opposite directions; *(2)* form a loop with one of the lines, as shown; *(3)* pass the free end through the loop and around the other line 4-5 times and then tighten; *(4)* repeat steps 2 and 3 with the other line; *(5)* pull on both lines to draw the two knots together and snug them up.

Tying a Bobber Stop—Sliding Stop

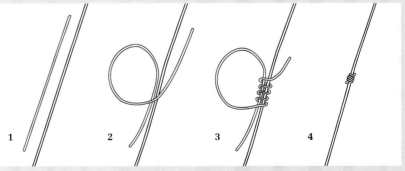

A sliding stop comes in handy for slip-bobber fishing and also has other uses, like marking your depth.

(1) Lay a foot-long piece of Nylon or Dacron line alongside your fishing line, *(2)* form a loop in the short line, as shown, *(3)* pass the free end of the short line through the loop and around the standing line 4-5 times, *(4)* pull on both ends of the short line to snug up the knot.

Attaching Mono to Wire—Albright Special

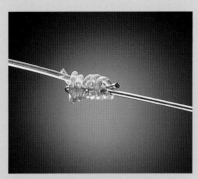

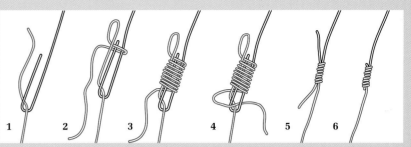

The Albright Special enables you to attach mono to wire or much heavier mono without a bulky barrel swivel.

(1) Double the wire, then pass the free end of the mono through the loop; *(2)* hold the mono alongside the wire and wrap the free end around the wire; *(3)* make 8 wraps, moving toward the loop in the wire; *(4)* pass the free end of the mono through the loop; *(5)* alternate pulling on the free end and standing line to snug up the knot; *(6)* trim wire and mono.

Attaching Hook or Lure to Wire Leader—Haywire Twist

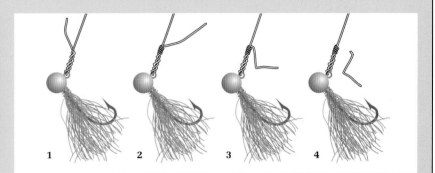

A haywire twist is a slick method for connecting a single-strand wire leader to a hook or lure. Don't try this with braided wire.

(1) Pass the wire through the eye of the lure or hook and make 3 loose twists; *(2)* make 5 tight wraps, winding the free end of the wire around the standing wire; *(3)* make a right-angle bend in the free end; *(4)* turn the "handle" until the excess wire breaks off.

Attaching Fly Line to Leader—Tube Knot

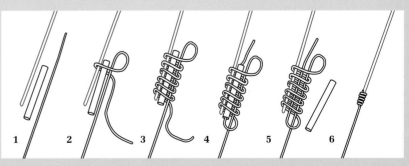

A tube knot makes a smooth connection between a fly line and leader.

(1) Lay a small plastic drinking straw alongside the end of the fly line; *(2)* wrap the leader butt around the fly line, straw and standing portion of the leader; *(3)* make about 5 wraps, winding toward the end of the fly line; *(4)* push the butt of the leader back through the straw; *(5)* carefully remove the straw; *(6)* pull on both ends of the leader to snug up the knot.

READING MAPS

If you know how to read a hydrographic map, you can gather loads of fishing information before you ever put your boat in the water. State or Federal agencies have surveyed practically every important fishing lake in the country, and maps showing bottom contours and other features important to anglers are available at a reasonable price.

A hydrographic map won't show you exactly where to fish, but it will give you a good idea of spots to check out with your depth finder. It will pinpoint features like small humps, sharp inside turns on the breaklines, extended lips of points and other spots that could be found only by hours of exploring.

If you're planning on fishing an unfamiliar lake, and you have a friend that commonly fishes there, ask him to mark a lake map for you. This will save you even more time.

Fishing maps with GPS coordinates are now starting to appear and will undoubtedly be the wave of the future. These maps take all the guesswork out of finding a productive fishing spot.

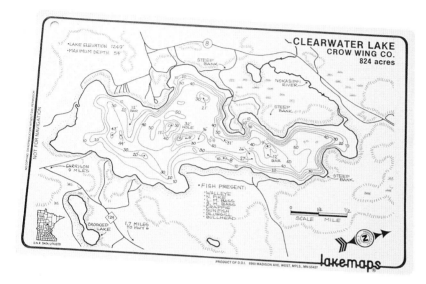

Hydrographic maps show the lake's structure with contour lines at regular depth intervals, usually 10 feet. Some maps also show bottom type, identifying rocky or weedy areas.

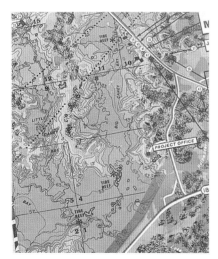

Reservoir maps not only show the bottom contour, they pinpoint the location of fish-attracting features such as old roadbeds, house foundations and stock ponds that existed before the lake filled.

GPS maps provide the exact latitude and longitude of good fishing spots. All the angler has to do is enter the coordinates in a GPS unit and navigate to the precise location.

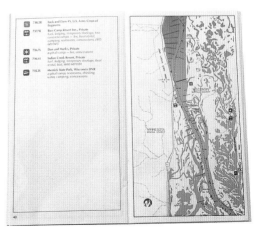

River charts show the location of features such as boat ramps, resorts, mileage markers, riprap banks, wing dams, side channels and dams. The Corps of Engineers publishes maps for most big rivers.

How to Read a Hydrographic Map

A gradually sloping break (A) appears as a series of widely spaced contour lines.

An inside bend (B) has contour lines opposite those of a point.

An underwater point (C) appears as a series of nearly parallel contour lines jutting out from shore.

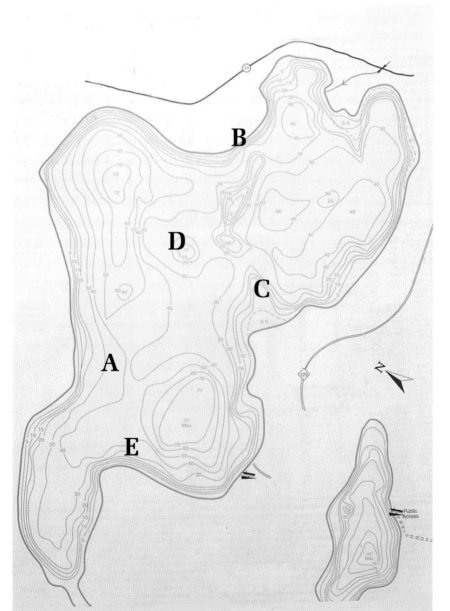

A hump (D) has a series of circular contour lines with the shallowest spot near the center.

A sharp-sloping break (E) appears as a series of closely spaced contour lines.

GETTING THE MOST FROM YOUR DEPTH FINDER

To get strong fish marks, your gain must be set properly. If it's set too low (left inset) the fish barely show up. If it's set too high, the screen will have too much "scatter" (right inset).

How to Get a Good High-Speed Reading

Place the transducer where there is a smooth flow of water under the boat. While the boat is running, look over the transom to find a slick spot (arrow); that's the best place for mounting your transducer.

Tilt the transducer back about 5 degrees so the water flow hits the transducer's face, which should be just slightly below the boat bottom. If the transducer's face is pointing straight down, there will be too much turbulence to get a good high-speed reading.

A good depth finder is the most valuable tool in your fishing boat but, to make the best use of it, you must set the transducer properly (opposite) and adjust the unit to suit the fishing situation.

Most liquid-crystals default to "automatic" to set your gain (power or sensitivity), depth range and chart speed. But automatic may not be best for your specific situation. That's why many experienced anglers prefer manual settings. In automatic, for example, the unit may give you a 0 to 40-foot depth scale in water 25 feet deep. But by manually setting the scale to 0 to 30 feet, or zooming in to 20 to 30 feet, you can better see what's happening below.

When sounding at high-speed, your chart speed should be set to maximum. Otherwise, any fish you graph will show up as tiny marks that may not even be noticeable.

At right are some tips for interpreting the signals your depth finder is sending you. Liquid-crystals are used in the examples, but the principles are the same for any kind of depth finder.

Interpreting Depth Finder Signals

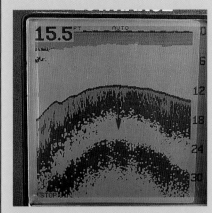

Hard bottom appears as a thick line with a sharp upper edge. If your gain is set high enough, you may also see a double echo at twice the depth (arrow).

Soft bottom (arrow) appears as a thin line with a fuzzy upper edge. Usually, there is no double echo.

Standing weeds, such as cabbage, appear as vertical columns coming up off the bottom.

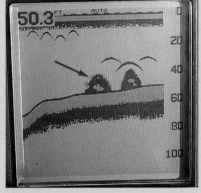

Baitfish schools (arrow) appear as clusters of tiny marks. If the school is tightly packed, it may just look like a solid clump.

A fish lying on bottom may look like a hump (blue arrow) with some open space or "air" underneath it. A rock (red arrow) looks similar, but has no air beneath it.

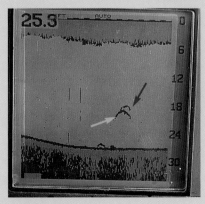

A large fish shows as a thick, black mark (blue arrow); a small fish, a thin, light one (red arrow). The length of the mark has little to do with the size of the fish.

GETTING THE MOST FROM YOUR GPS

A GPS navigator does a lot more than just navigate. For example, you can use it as an "invisible marker," a trolling-speed indicator or a mapping device for plotting the shape of the structure you're fishing.

Some GPS units even have a "man overboard" feature that enables you to instantly mark the spot where you dropped a fishing rod – or a passenger – into the water.

Here are some basic GPS guidelines, along with some tips for using GPS to put a few extra fish into your boat.

Navigation Basics

Push the waypoint key and then punch in the latitude and longitude of a waypoint (spot) that you got from a map or from a fishing friend. When the numbers are entered, assign the waypoint a number and give it a name, so you will be able to recognize it on your waypoint log. You can also enter a waypoint you've just found by pressing "quick save".

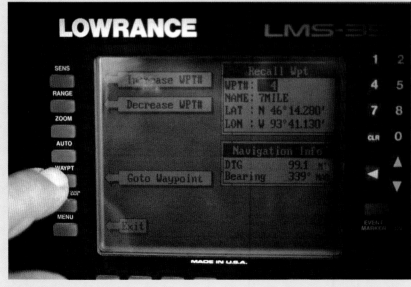

Recall the waypoint from your log and push "go to waypoint". The unit will give you the bearing and distance to the waypoint and, while you're moving, tell how far you are to the side of a straight line to the waypoint (XTE or cross-track error).

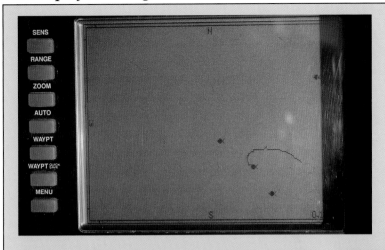

When you locate fish, put fish "icons" on the screen of your GPS; this way, you can keep your boat in the vicinity of the school.

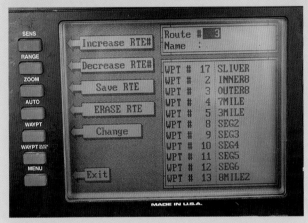

To navigate on waters where you can't travel in a straight line, such as an island-studded lake, make a route consisting of several waypoints. When you reach the first waypoint, the unit will automatically switch to the second and tell you how to get there.

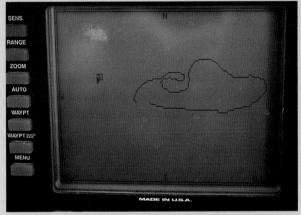

Map out the structure you're fishing by putting the unit in plotter mode. Set the plotter's range to match the size of the piece of structure. Just follow the edge of the structure with your depth finder and the plotter will map its shape.

Mapping modules are available for most of the United States and Canada. These modules make navigation easier, because you can see points, islands and other features in relation to the path of the boat. Some maps even show bottom contours.

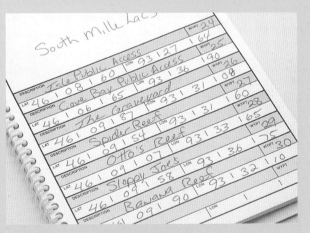

Keep a log book listing all of your important waypoints. This way, should your unit's waypoint log get erased, your waypoints won't be lost forever. You can buy waypoint logs printed on heavy, waterproof paper.

BOAT CONTROL

Backtroll into the wind for precise boat control. Splash guards will prevent waves from lapping into your boat. The reason backtrolling allows such precision is that the wind doesn't affect your transom as much as your bow. And, with your depth finder's transducer mounted right next to your motor, it's easy to follow a contour.

Boat control has been referred to as "the little-known secret of big-time anglers." If you can't keep your boat on the fish, all the best equipment and hottest new lures won't matter.

Whether you're trolling, drifting or anchoring, boat control is an important issue.

If you have a deep-hulled boat, backtrolling (above) is your best option. If you try to troll forward, the wind will catch the bow and blow you

Controlling Your Drift

Use your trolling motor to control your drift path. If you're trying to follow a contour, and the wind is blowing you closer to shore, keep kicking the boat out with the motor to stay at the right depth.

Toss out a drift sock to slow your drift on a windy day. The bigger the sock you use, the more it will slow you down. To pull a drift sock in quickly and easily, attach a rope to the narrow end.

Anchoring Tips

Prevent your anchor from slipping by using a heavier anchor than you think you'll need and attaching about 6 feet of heavy chain to it. The chain lowers the angle of pull, so the flukes dig in.

Let out plenty of rope to further reduce the angle of pull. As a rule, the length of your anchor rope should be at least four times the water depth.

When anchoring on a windy day or in a current, turn the handle of your outboard to adjust the lateral position of the boat. Turning the handle to the left will push the boat to the right and vice versa.

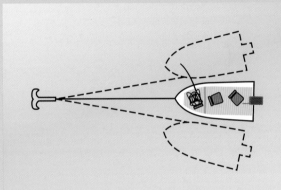

Changing your tie-off point will also adjust the lateral position of the boat. If you're tied off to the bow, for example, you can move the boat a few feet to the right by tying to the left-front cleat.

off course. If you own a low-profile bass boat, however, the bow is not affected as much by the wind, so forward trolling may work fine. Either way, always troll into the wind, straight or at an angle, for the best boat control.

A powerful electric trolling motor is the best investment a troller can make. By using a motor with half again as much thrust as is recommended for your boat, you can make course corrections much faster and spend more of your time fishing where the fish are.

A powerful trolling motor is also a big help in drifting. Seldom does the wind blow you in exactly the direction you want to go. With a hefty trolling motor, you can keep your boat on the desired drift path and control your drift speed.

Another handy tool for drifting is a sea anchor, or drift sock. Some anglers use two of them, one off the bow and one off the stern, to slow their drift in windy weather. A drift sock also helps control the boat while trolling; not only does it slow you

down, it keeps the bow from swinging in the wind.

Anchoring is a subject you hear very little about, but it's by far the best way to stay on a tight school of fish. If you repeatedly trolled or drifted over them, you'd probably spook them. But you must know how to anchor in exactly the right spot, with no chance of your anchor slipping and dragging right through the school of fish.

Take some time to study the boat-control tips on these pages. They're sure to make a big difference in your fishing.

FISHING TECHNIQUES

This chapter will acquaint you with the most important species of freshwater gamefish found in North America. Besides expaining the key points of their biology of importance to anglers, we'll also show you the spots where they're most likely to be found and the most popular techniques for catching them.

LARGEMOUTH BASS

Micropterus salmoides

The largemouth bass is America's favorite gamefish — and for good reason. It is found in all of the lower 48 states and its range extends from southern Canada to Mexico and Cuba.

But widespread distribution is not the only reason for its popularity. The largemouth is a willing biter, eagerly attacking practically any kind of artificial lure or live bait. And once you get one on the end of your line, you'll know what all the fuss is about. A hooked bass will jump, sizzle off line, try to wrap you around weeds and otherwise carry on like few other gamefish.

Largemouth Facts

Largemouth bass belong to the sunfish family and are classified as warmwater fish. Although they can survive near-freezing temperatures, they do very little feeding when the water dips below 50°F.

There are two subspecies of largemouth bass: the northern largemouth and the Florida largemouth. They look nearly identical, the only difference being that the scales are a little smaller on the Florida bass. The latter, which were originally found only in the Florida Peninsula, grow much faster and reach a considerably larger size than northern bass, with several 20-plus pounders on record. The giant bass currently being caught in California, Texas and Mexico are Florida largemouths.

You can find largemouth in weedy natural lakes, reservoirs with plenty of woody cover, sluggish streams and small ponds or pits that do not freeze out in winter. They can tolerate water clarity

Largemouth bass range.

Largemouth bass are greenish to tannish in color with a darker back, lighter belly and a dark horizontal band. The jaw is longer than that of the smallmouth, extending past the rear of the eye.

ranging from only a few inches to 20 feet or more. They are more salt-tolerant than most freshwater fish, which explains why they are found in tidewater rivers. The largemouth's preferred temperature range is 68 to 78°F.

Largemouth may well be the least-selective feeders of all freshwater fish. The bulk of their diet includes a variety of small fish, including their own young, crayfish and larval aquatic insects, but they also eat small mammals, salamanders, frogs, worms, leeches, snails, turtles and even small snakes.

When the water warms to the lower 60s in spring, male largemouths move into the shallows to begin building their nests. They normally nest in a bay or along a shoreline that is sheltered from the wind, usually around weedy or woody cover. Using his tail, the male fans away silt to reach a firm sandy or gravelly bottom, then the female moves in to deposit her eggs. By the time the water reaches the upper 60s, most spawning is completed. The male guards the nest and remains with the fry until they disperse.

Largemouth have been known to live as long as 16 years, but it is unusual for them to live for more than 10. Although the growth rate of Florida bass far exceeds that of northern bass, Floridas stocked in the North grow no faster than the native bass. An 8-year-old northern largemouth typically weighs about 5 pounds; a Florida of the same age, about 10 pounds.

Key Largemouth Locations...

In Natural Lakes
Early Spring:
- Shallow mud-bottomed bays, channels and harbors that warm earliest

Spawning Time:
- Protected bays and shorelines with a firm bottom

Summer and Early Fall:
- Weedlines, humps and points that have weedy or rocky cover and slope gradually into deep water
- Slop bays, where dense overhead vegetation keeps the water cooler

Slop bay

Late Fall and Winter:
- Points, humps and other structure that slopes rapidly into deep water
- Inside turns along breaklines
- Shallow flats on warm days

In Man-Made Lakes
Early Spring thru Spawning:
- Back ends of shallow, brushy creek arms

Brushy creek arm

Late Spring and Summer:
- Main lake points adjacent to the old river channel
- Bends and intersections in the old river channel or in deep creek channels
- Humps with standing timber or submerged weeds
- Timbered flats

Early Fall:
- Back ends of creek arms

Late Fall and Winter:
- Deep main-lake points
- Main river channels

In Rivers
Early Spring thru Spawning:
- Shallow, dead-end sloughs and other backwaters off the main river
- Shallow sandbars
- Stump fields

Late Spring to Early Fall:
- Sloughs with current
- Deep backwaters
- Side channels into backwaters

Side channel

- Wingdams
- Deep eddies and outside bends
- Undercut banks and ledges

Late Fall and Winter:
- Deep areas of main channels
- Deep holes in backwaters
- Near warmwater discharges

Largemouth Bass Techniques

Largemouth bite best when water temperatures are in the 60s and 70s. They're most active under dim-light conditions. On bright, sunny days, they usually tuck into dense cover, where it's difficult to get a lure to them. They do most of their feeding early and late in the day. On cloudy days, they roam farther from cover and feed throughout the day. An approaching storm often triggers a flurry of feeding, but the action slows dramatically following a cold front.

Good largemouth fishermen are versatile. There are times when the fish want topwaters and times when they want a spoon jigged in 50 feet of water. Perhaps the most important consideration in selecting lures is the type of cover. In heavy weeds, for instance, you need a spinnerbait, Texas-rigged worm, weedless jig or other bait that won't foul or hang up. On a clean bottom, you're better off with a bait that has open hooks. On the pages that follow, we'll

The plastic worm is the number-one bass producer.

acquaint you with the major largemouth techniques used across North America.

Fishing Soft Plastics

Soft plastics are a favorite of largemouth anglers nationwide. Not only do they look and feel like real food, they can be rigged Texas-style (with the hook point buried in the worm), so they can be fished in the densest cover.

When fishing soft plastics on a clean bottom, many anglers prefer to use a Carolina rig with an open hook. With a slip-sinker attached well up the line, the lure sinks more slowly and

has a more enticing action than a Texas-rigged bait. Some anglers use sinkers weighing up to 1 ounce, enabling them to make very long casts and cover more water. When a bass picks up the bait, the line slips through the sinker, so the fish feels no resistance.

Another popular option for fishing on a clean bottom or in sparse weeds is rigging the lure on a light jig head.

Soft plastics are normally fished quite slowly, so they work best when you have a pretty good idea of where the fish are located. They are not a good choice for exploring new water.

Recommended Tackle

The type of tackle you use for largemouth depends mainly on the type of cover you're fishing. When casting a curlytail grub on a clean bottom, you can get by with a light spinning outfit and 6-pound monofilament. But when working a jig-and-pig in a dense weedbed or tree top, you'll need a heavy flippin' stick spooled with mono or superline of at least 20-pound test.

Types of Soft Plastics

slug

lizard

ribbontail worm

curlytail worm

straight-tail worm

craw

paddletail worm

French Fry

reaper

weenie worm

Because they are retrieved so slowly, soft plastics are effective in cold water or at other times when bass are lethargic and unwilling to chase fast-moving baits. But they also work well in warm water.

You can retrieve a soft plastic with a slow, steady crawl, hop it along the bottom with a jigging motion, or even reel it rapidly on or just beneath the surface. The only way to determine what retrieve works best is to experiment.

When bass are finicky, it may take a super-slow presentation with a light spinning outfit and a small bait to draw a strike. Try rigging a 3- or 4-inch soft plastic on a plain hook with only a split-shot for weight and then inching the rig along the bottom. This technique is called "finesse fishing."

Always watch the line and rod tip closely. If you see a twitch, feel a "tick," notice the line moving off to the side or detect anything out of the ordinary, point the rod tip at the bait and reel up slack until you start to feel the weight of the fish. Then, set the hook with a strong upward sweep of the rod.

A bass will usually hold on to a soft plastic bait for several seconds before it lets go. Some anglers prefer to hesitate for a few seconds before setting the hook; others say you should set right away. If you're rigging Texas-style, it takes an extra-hard hookset to drive the hook though the plastic and into the bass' jaw.

Popular Rigging Methods

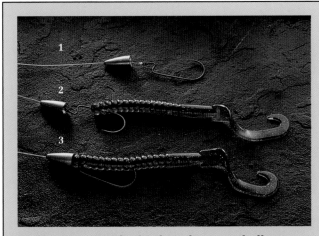

Make a Texas rig by *(1)* threading on a bullet sinker and then attaching an offset worm hook. *(2)* Push the hook into the bait about ³/₈ inch, then bring it out the side. *(3)* Twist the hook 180 degrees and then push the point back into the bait so it almost, but not quite, comes out the opposite side.

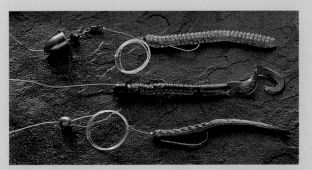

Top: *Make a Carolina rig with a straight worm hook, brass sinker and glass bead. The "brass and glass" creates a loud clicking noise that bass love.*
Center: *Rig a soft-plastic on a mushroom-head jig. Mushroom heads are a good choice because they butt up flush with the bait, leaving no gap to catch weeds.*
Bottom: *Rig a small grub or a "weenie" worm on a thin-wire hook with a single split-shot.*

Hang a weighted minnowbait, or "jerkbait," in a largemouth's face to tempt a strike. This technique works best during coldwater periods or whenever the fish are lethargic.

at the depth you want to fish.

Crankbaits were once considered warmwater lures because, in cold water, bass were too lethargic to chase them. But anglers have discovered that they work well in cold water when fished with a slow, stop-and-go retrieve.

Minnowbaits are long and slim, with a narrow lip that gives them more of a wiggle than a wobble. They generally run shallower than crankbaits, although some long-lipped models dive deep. Some of these lures are weighted to make them neutrally buoyant. This way, you can stop your retrieve and hang the bait in a fish's face (left) without it floating up.

Vibrating plugs don't have a lip; the attachment eye is on the back. These baits have a very tight wiggle and, because they sink, can be fished at any depth.

Fishing Subsurface Plugs

Subsurface plugs make it possible to cover a lot of water in a hurry, even when the bass are deep. And a largemouth finds the enticing wiggle hard to resist.

The three main types of subsurface plugs used in largemouth fishing are crankbaits, minnowbaits and vibrating plugs.

Crankbaits have a relatively short, deep body and a broad lip that gives them a wide wobble. Some dive to depths of 30 feet; others run only a few feet

beneath the surface. You need to select a bait that runs

Rat-L-Trap (vibrating plug)

Down Deep Rattlin' Fat Rap (deep-diving crankbait)

Norman Little N (shallow-running crankbait)

Thunderstick (minnowbait)

Spinnerbait Fishing

A spinnerbait is a good choice for largemouths in heavy cover. You can toss it into weeds or brush and not worry about it hanging up or fouling, because the spinner shaft acts as a weedguard for the upturned single hook.

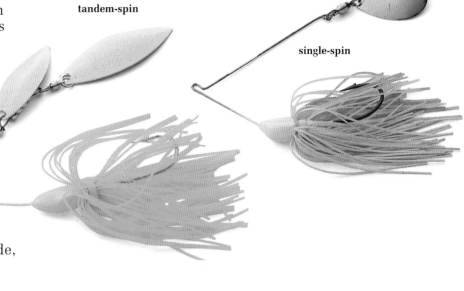

tandem-spin

single-spin

There are two basic types of spinner-baits. Single-spins, which have only one blade, are a good all-around choice and work well for helicoptering. The blade spins easily as the bait sinks.

Tandem-spins have a pair of blades that give the bait extra lift. They're the best choice for fishing over shallow weed tops or for other shallow-water presentations.

The performance of a spinnerbait is also affected by the type of blade(s). Colorado blades have the most water resistance, so they provide the most lift. The blade spins easily on a slow retrieve. Willow-leaf blades have less water resistance, so they can be fished faster and deeper.

Although spinnerbaits are generally considered shallow-water baits, heavy models ($3/4$ ounce or more) work well in water as deep as 30 feet. If you need a little extra depth, add a pinch-on sinker to the bait's lower arm or hook shank.

For extra attraction, many anglers tip their spinnerbaits with a pork frog or a soft-plastic grub.

Popular Spinnerbait Retrieves

Slow-roll a spinnerbait by reeling slowly and allowing it to bump bottom or the top of weedy or brushy cover.

Reel your spinnerbait to the edge of vertical cover, like a tree or breakwall, and let it helicopter down to reach tight-holding bass.

Bulge a spinnerbait by keeping your rod tip high and reeling fast enough that the blades almost break the surface.

Jigging

Jigging for largemouth can be done with a variety of baits, primarily lead-head jigs and jigging spoons.

Lead-head jigs are available in many different head shapes, each serving a certain purpose. Jigs are tied with or tipped with various dressings, including hair, feathers, rubber skirts or soft-plastic trailers.

Technically, the term "jigging" means working your bait with a rapid up-and-down motion. But jigs are not necessarily fished that way. More often, they're just inched along the bottom.

Jigging spoons have a heavy body and sink rapidly, so they're ideal for jigging bass in deep water. Some anglers use them to fish in depths of 50 feet or more. With their long, thin shape, they look like an injured minnow.

If you get snagged in heavy cover, just let your line go slack. The weight of the spoon usually pulls the hook free.

A jig-and-pig is hard to beat when bass are tucked into heavy cover.

Popular Types of Jigs & Jigging Baits

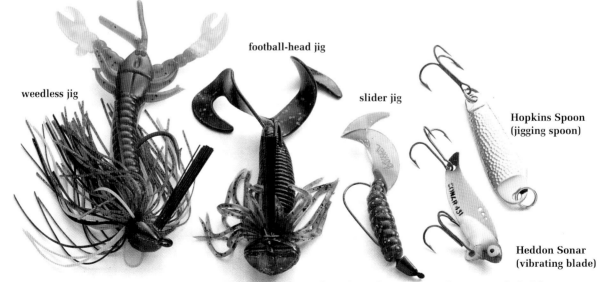

weedless jig

football-head jig

slider jig

Hopkins Spoon (jigging spoon)

Heddon Sonar (vibrating blade)

Use a weedless jig to avoid hang-ups in dense weeds or brush; a football jig for a crayfish-like, tip-up action on a rocky bottom; a slider jig for working the weed tops; and a vibrating blade or jigging spoon for vertically jigging in deep water.

Types of Topwaters

Blue Fox Black Flash (buzzbait)

Snagproof Tournament Frog

Lucky 13 (chugger)

Zara Spook (stickbait)

Jitterbug (crawler)

Dying Flutter (propbait)

Topwater Fishing

To many anglers, an explosive surface strike is the ultimate fishing thrill. And when conditions are right, largemouth bass are one of the most cooperative surface feeders.

Topwaters are most effective when the surface is calm and the water temperature exceeds 60°F. They work best early or late in the day or at night but, when the fish are in heavy cover, they'll hit topwaters in the middle of the day. Largemouth anglers use practically every kind of bait that floats for topwater fishing.

Stickbaits, long, thin plugs with no built-in action, are weighted in the tail to give them a side-to-side action.

Propbaits look like stickbaits, but they have propellers at one or both ends. They're normally fished with twitches followed by pauses.

Chuggers have a concave or flat face that throws water when you jerk. They're often retrieved with a series of rapid twitches.

Crawlers have a broad face plate or arms that make the bait wobble or crawl. A slow, steady retrieve usually works best.

Buzzbaits have a large blade that throws a lot of water. Retrieve them slowly and steadily; they'll sink if you stop reeling.

Frogs and rats are made of soft rubber or plastic and have a weedless design. They are the best choice for fishing heavily matted weeds.

Popular Topwater Retrieves

A twitch-and-pause retrieve can be used with most topwaters, but it works especially well with propbaits and chuggers. The latter can also be fished using a rapid series of twitches, with no pauses.

Retrieve a stickbait by holding your rod tip low and giving it a series of evenly-spaced jerks to make the head swing from one side to the other. This retrieve is called "walking the dog."

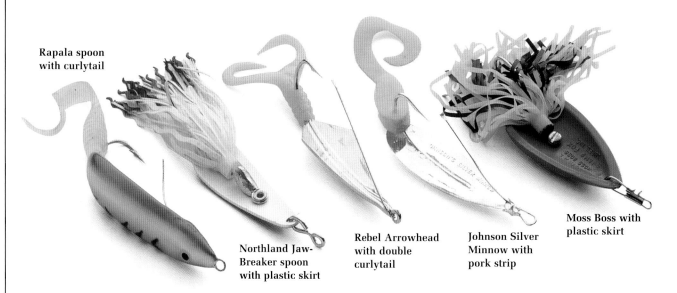

Rapala spoon
with curlytail

Northland Jaw-
Breaker spoon
with plastic skirt

Rebel Arrowhead
with double
curlytail

Johnson Silver
Minnow with
pork strip

Moss Boss with
plastic skirt

Fishing Weedless Spoons

A weedless spoon, with its wire or nylon bristle weed-guard, can slither its way through the densest weedbed. And, when tipped with a pork strip or plastic trailer, the bait has an incredibly lifelike swimming action.

Although weedless spoons are not as popular as they once were, they are still an important tool for anglers who do a lot of fishing in heavy vegetation or brushy cover.

Some weedless spoons are made of metal; others, hard plastic. Metal spoons, because they are heavier, work best for fan-casting large expanses of weedy cover. They sink rapidly and are fished beneath the surface.

Hard-plastic spoons are light enough to slide over matted weeds. Because they ride with the hook up, there is little chance of fouling.

One drawback to the weedless spoon is the tendency for fish to strike short. Many anglers make the mistake of setting the hook when they feel a bass nip at the trailer. Be sure to hesitate until you feel the weight of the fish before setting.

The Skitter-and-Drop Retrieve

1 Make a long cast and start your retrieve before the lure can sink. Keep your rod tip high and reel just fast enough so the spoon skitters over the weeds or runs just beneath the surface.

2 Stop reeling when you come to a pocket in the weeds. Drop your rod tip to let the spoon sink into the pocket. That's when a bass that has been tracking the spoon will strike.

Fly Fishing

Not only is fly fishing for largemouth a lot of fun, there are times when it is one of the most effective bass-catching methods.

When bass are in shallow water, the chugging action of a bass bug draws their attention from a considerable distance. And when they spot the hairy bug, they're almost sure to grab it.

Besides bass bugs, fly fishermen use poppers, big streamers, crayfish patterns and leech imitations to catch largemouth. If you'll be fishing in dense cover, you'll need a fly with a wire or mono weedguard.

Recommended tackle includes a 7- to 9-weight fly rod with a floating, weight-forward or bass-bug taper line, for punching the heavy flies into the wind. Use a 6- to 9-foot leader with a 0X to 4X tippet.

A mono weedguard prevents most hang-ups, yet is flexible enough that it doesn't interfere with your hookset.

Popular Bass Flies

Wiggle-Legs Frog

deer-hair popper

Dahlberg Diver

wool streamer

Blackhare Leech

SMALLMOUTH BASS

Micropterus dolomieui

If you ask a well-travelled angler to name the fightingest freshwater fish, the smallmouth bass will most likely get the nod.

Known for its aerial antics, a smallmouth almost always heads straight for the surface when it feels the hook. It explodes out of the water, fiercely shaking its head in an attempt to throw the bait. If it doesn't succeed on the first jump, it will try several more times. Some anglers have even had a smallmouth jump into their boat!

Smallmouth Facts

Like its close cousin, the largemouth, the smallmouth belongs to the sunfish family and is considered a warmwater fish. However, smallmouth lean slightly toward the coolwater category. They prefer water in the 67- to 71-degree range, although they're sometimes caught at temperatures in the low 80s. Feeding slows considerably when the water temperature drops below 50°F, and stops altogether at about 40.

There are two recognized subspecies of smallmouth bass. The northern smallmouth (*Micropterus dolomieui dolomieui*) is, by far, the most common. The Neosho smallmouth *(Micropterus dolomieui velox)* has been nearly wiped out by construction of dams on its native waters.

Smallmouths are found in most types of natural lakes and reservoirs as well as in rivers and streams with moderate current. They rarely inhabit small ponds, shallow lakes, sluggish streams or any muddy or badly polluted water. They prefer a hard bottom, usually rock or gravel, and are seldom found on a soft, mucky bottom.

Spawning takes place in spring, usually at water temperatures in the 60- to 65-degree range. The male selects a spawning site on a sand-gravel or rock bottom in a protected area, often next to a boulder or log. He fans the silt from the bottom with his tail, then the female moves in to deposit her eggs. After spawning is completed, the male stays on the nest to guard the eggs and, later, the fry.

Smallmouth are especially fond of crayfish, but they also eat a variety of other foods, including frogs, insect larvae, adult insects and many kinds of minnows and other small fish. As a rule, they prefer smaller food items than largemouth, explaining why anglers generally use smaller baits.

In the North, smallmouth bass may live as long as 18 years. They rarely live half that long in the South, but

Smallmouth have a jaw extending to the middle of the eye. They are greenish to bronze in color, accounting for their common name, bronzeback. They have dark vertical bars or diamond patterns on the side, but these marks are not always present and may come and go. The cheek also has dark bars. The eye is often reddish.

Smallmouth bass range.

they grow considerably faster. It takes about 8 years for a smallmouth in northern waters to reach 3 pounds, and only 4 years to achieve the same weight in the South.

Fishing Techniques

If you've ever reeled in a smallmouth and spotted several more following it, attempting to take away its meal, you know how aggressive these fish can be.

That type of behavior is most often seen on lightly fished waters. But where fishing pressure is heavy, the fish are a lot more selective.

There are times when smallmouth will grab big baits, but they generally prefer baits a little smaller than those normally used for largemouth. Many smallmouth lures, like jigs and crankbaits, are intended to mimic crayfish and are available in crayfish colors. But don't get too hung up on the crayfish connection. Smallmouth will hit many other kinds of lures, as well, including minnowbaits, in-line spinners, spinnerbaits and topwaters.

Although size and action of a bait is more important than color, most smallmouth

Recommended Tackle

On clean structure, a medium-power spinning outfit with 6- to 8-pound mono is adequate for most presentations. In heavier cover, a medium- to medium-heavy-power baitcasting outfit with 10- to 14-pound mono is a better choice.

anglers opt for dark or drab colors rather than bright or fluorescent hues.

When fishing is tough, live bait is the best option. Crayfish, especially softshells, are hard to beat, but many anglers swear by hellgrammites (dobson-fly larvae). Other good baits include shiners, nightcrawlers and leeches. Present these baits on a slip-sinker or slip-bobber rig, just as you would for walleyes (pp.126-128). Or simply fish them on a plain hook with only a split-shot for weight.

Although smallmouth are good to eat, we strongly urge you to release them. Because of their willingness to bite, they can easily be overfished. And their value on the end of a fishing line far outweighs their value on a dinner plate.

Key Locations for Smallmouth Bass...

In Natural Lakes

Early Spring through Spawning:
- Sheltered sand-gravel bays
- Bulrush beds adjacent to deep water
- Shallow points with scattered boulders for cover

Point with scattered boulders

Late Spring through Early Fall:
- Gradually tapering points with a sandy, gravelly or rocky bottom
- Mouths of major inlets, particularly in shield lakes

Tributary stream

- Rocky reefs in lakes with a sandy bottom
- Sandy, weedy humps in lakes with a rocky bottom
- Sandy bays in rocky lakes
- Flats adjacent to deep water with rocks, logs or scattered weeds for cover

Late Fall and Winter:
- Steep-sloping points
- Irregular breaklines that drop rapidly into deep water
- Deep gravel or rock humps

In Man-Made Lakes

Early Spring:
- Creek arms with flowing inlet streams
- Shallow secondary creek arms

Spring (spawning):
- Rocky shorelines in protected creek arms
- Shallow, rocky points in the main lake

Summer and Early Fall:
- Rocky reefs or sandy humps, especially those near the old river channel
- Timbered flats along the old river channel (nighttime feeding area)

Timbered flat

- Rock slides along steep canyon walls (canyon reservoirs)
- Long points extending into the old river channel

Extended point

- Man-made fish attractors

Late Fall and Winter:
- Deep main-lake points
- Deep inside turns along the old river channel
- Eddies in tailrace areas

In Rivers

Early Spring through Spawning:
- Tributaries with a rocky bottom draw smallmouth if there are few rock areas in the river itself
- Shallow gravel shoals
- Backwaters with some moving water
- Shallow, riprapped banks

Summer and Early Fall:
- Eddies below rocky points
- Deep pools below riffles
- Steep ledges along limestone banks
- Wingdams

Wingdam

- Deep riprap along shorelines and islands
- Eddies below boulders
- Side channels connecting the main channel and backwater areas
- Eddies alongside the swift water below a low-head dam

Late Fall and Winter:
- Deep holes in the main river channel that have very little or no current
- Warmwater discharges

Eddy below low-head dam

Jigging

The lead-head jig is arguably the deadliest of all smallmouth baits. You can inch it along a rocky bottom to mimic a crayfish or minnow and, because of the upturned hook, it's less likely to snag than most other baits.

Lead-head jigs are dressed with hair or feathers or tipped with a rubber skirt, soft-plastic grub or live bait (usually a leech, minnow or piece of nightcrawler). The fly n' rind (a hair jig with a pork trailer) is a popular smallmouth bait throughout much of the South.

Another effective smallmouth technique is vertical jigging using a variety of jigging lures, including jigging spoons, tailspinners and vibrating blades. You can also jig vertically with a lead-head jig. In deep, clear, southern reservoirs, anglers vertical jig for smallmouth in water more than 40 feet deep.

Vertical jigging is a simple technique, but there's a trick to it. Give your rod a quick snap to lift the bait, then follow the line back down with your rod tip, keeping the line slightly taut, but not tight. Nine times out of ten, the bass will grab the bait as it is sinking and, if your line is not taut, you won't feel a thing. When you feel a tap, bump or anything out of the ordinary, set the hook.

A jig tipped with a smoke grub is a top smallmouth producer.

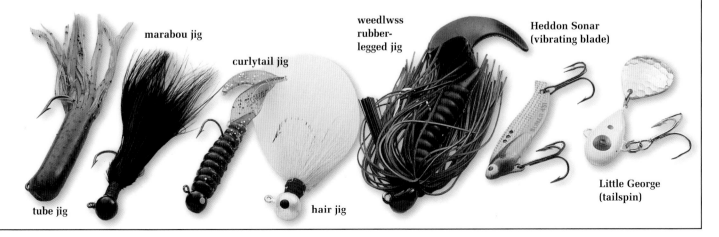

marabou jig

curlytail jig

weedlwss rubber-legged jig

Heddon Sonar (vibrating blade)

tube jig

hair jig

Little George (tailspin)

Subsurface Plugs

Serious smallmouth anglers carry a good supply of crankbaits, minnowbaits and vibrating plugs. With these baits, you can cover a lot of water quickly to locate active fish. Then, after the bite slows down, you can switch to a slower bait, like a jig, and work the area more thoroughly.

Plugs used for smallmouth are usually 2 to 3 inches long, a little smaller than those used for largemouth. Although crayfish colors (browns and oranges) are most popular, shad and shiner colors are equally effective.

As a rule, minnowbaits, with their tighter wiggle, work better than crankbaits when the water is cool. They're also a good choice at spawning time. Fish them on the surface with a twitch-and-pause retrieve.

Crankbaits and vibrating plugs are excellent summertime baits and are a better choice for fishing deep structure.

Vibrating plugs are proven smallmouth baits.

Rebel Deep Wee-R
(crankbait)

Rattlin' Rap
(vibrating plug)

Rebel Floating Minnow (minnowbait)

Spinnerbaits

Most anglers think of a spinnerbait as a dynamite shallow-water lure for largemouth, but few consider using it for smallmouth.

But that's a big mistake, especially when the fish are in weedy cover. Spinnerbaits also excel for night fishing in clear lakes. The thumping blades draw smallmouths up to the surface from deep water, often from depths of 20 or 30 feet.

Although ⅛- to ⅜-ounce spinnerbaits are the usual choice of smallmouth fishermen, some savvy anglers have found that heavy spinnerbaits (¾- to 1-ounce models) work well for deepwater smallmouth. Just slow-roll the bait across a deep rock pile or other deep-water structure, or let it helicopter straight down a cliff wall or a steep channel break.

For extra attraction, try tipping your spinnerbait with a soft-plastic grub. The rapidly wiggling tail may double the number of strikes.

In-Line Spinners

These simple baits don't get much press, but when smallmouth are cruising a rocky shoreline or other shallow, clean-bottomed structure, an in-line spinner works exceptionally well. Because of its open hooks, this bait is not a good choice in weeds or brush.

In-line spinners come with two different styles of blades. A standard blade is attached to a clevis, which spins around the shaft. A sonic blade spins directly on the shaft. The latter is concave at one end and spins at a lower retrieve speed. A size 2 or 3 blade usually works best for smallmouth.

There isn't much skill involved in fishing an in-line spinner; you just cast it out and reel it in. Retrieve just fast enough to keep the blade spinning.

One drawback to in-line spinners is that the whole bait tends to spin when you retrieve, badly twisting your line. You can solve the problem by attaching the bait with a snap swivel. Or, just bend the front of the shaft at about a 30-degree angle, creating a keel effect (right).

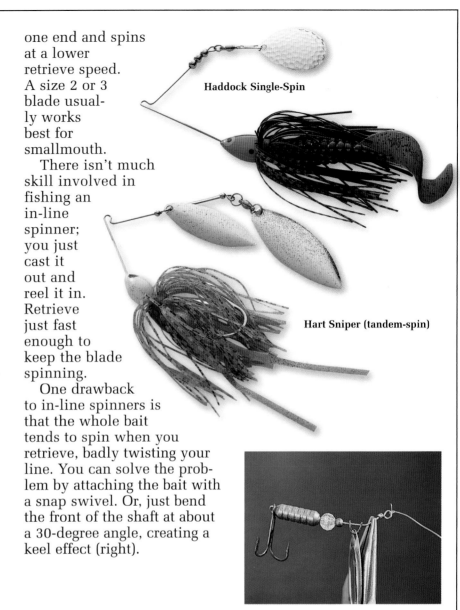

Haddock Single-Spin

Hart Sniper (tandem-spin)

A slight bend keeps the bait from spinning.

Blue Fox (standard)

Panther Martin (sonic)

Topwaters

One of the hottest new smallmouth techniques is using topwater baits to "call up" smallmouth from deep water. The technique works best in clear-water lakes, where anglers have been successful in calling the fish up from as deep as 30 feet. Some smallmouth experts have found this method to be even more effective at night.

Topwaters normally work best in spring, when smallmouth are cruising the shallows in preparation for spawning. They're feeding heavily and will take most any kind of topwater offering, including propbaits, chuggers, stickbaits and high-floating minnowbaits.

It may take a little experimentation to find the right retrieve. Sometimes twitches followed by long pauses work best; other times, the fish seem to like a series of rapid twitches with no pauses.

Floating Rapala
(stickbait)

Rebel Super
(Pop-R) chugger

Heddon Tiny
Torpedo (propbait)

Floating Rapala
(minnowbait)

Berkley Power Sand Worm

Toledo Tackle lizard

Berkley Power Leech

Luck "E" Strike
Baby Guido Bug

Luck "E" Strike G4 tube rigged on HP hook

Soft Plastics

You can buy soft-plastic baits that are near-perfect imitations of some of the smallmouth's favorite foods, such as crayfish, hellgrammites and lizards. The baits can be Texas-rigged for fishing in heavy cover, or Carolina-rigged for fishing on a clean bottom. Another good choice is a soft-plastic leech. These flattened baits have ripples molded into them so they undulate in leech-like fashion.

But exact imitations are seldom necessary to pique the interest of a smallmouth. You'll get plenty of strikes on plastic worms, as well. Most smallmouth anglers opt for worms from 4 to 6 inches long.

In recent years, tube baits have emerged as one of the top all-around smallmouth lures. Their slim profile and wiggling tentacles seem to be just what the fish want.

You can rig a tube bait on a jig head for fishing in deep water, or fish it weighted or unweighted on a weedless HP hook.

Fly Fishing

Smallmouth feed heavily on larval aquatic insects and, to a lesser extent, on adult forms, so it's not surprising that fly fishing is so effective. Many other fly patterns are intended to mimic hellgrammites, crayfish, leeches and shiner minnows – all smallmouth favorites.

While there is no denying the effectiveness of these realistic subsurface flies, many fishermen find "bugging" a lot more exciting.

The best bugs are made of clipped deer or elk hair. They float high on the surface, and when a smallmouth grabs one, it's not likely to let go, because the fly feels like real food. Perhaps the most popular of all bugs is the diver, which floats at rest

Muddler Minnow

crayfish

Woolley Bugger

Hare Sculpin

cork popper

deer-hair swimming frog

Clauser Minnow

but dives when you strip line (below).

A 6- to 8-weight fly rod with a matching weight-forward or bass-bug taper line is a good choice for smallmouth. Use a 6- to 9-foot, 2X to 5X leader and a size 1 to 6 fly.

How to Fish a Diver

After making a cast, strip line rapidly to make the fly dive.

Hesitate after stripping line; the hair traps air and when the fly is pulled under, an air bubble floats to the surface.

The action and gurgling sound draw many strikes, but don't set the hook until you feel the weight of the fish.

CATFISH

If you've ever wondered why catfish are so popular, consider these facts:
• Catfish reach weights of 50 to 100 pounds.
• The table quality of catfish is excellent.
• Catfish are powerful fighters.
• Catfish are within easy reach of the vast majority of North American anglers.

Originally, no catfish were found west of the Rockies, but stocking programs have greatly expanded their range.

Channel, flathead and blue catfish are the species most commonly sought by anglers. But white catfish are also popular in certain areas along the east and west coasts. Whites are considerably smaller than the other species, seldom exceeding 5 pounds.

Catfish are easy to recognize because of their whiskers, or *barbels*; their smooth, scaleless skin; and the *adipose* fin on their backs.

Catfish Facts

Catfish are classified as warmwater gamefish, preferring water temperatures from the mid 70s to mid 80s. They're found naturally in large warmwater rivers, including large tributaries of those waters, and have been stocked in many lakes and ponds. Catfish can tolerate muddy water but, contrary to popular belief, cannot survive where pollution levels are high or dissolved oxygen levels, low. Blue cats prefer clearer, faster water than the other catfish species.

Catfish spawn in late spring or early summer, when the water temperature is in the low to mid 70s. One or both of the parents build a nest in the shade of a log or boulder or in other dark, secluded areas, such as holes in the bank or sunken barrels. The male guards the nest until the fry are ready to leave.

Many anglers believe that catfish feed mainly on dead or rotting food, explaining

The channel catfish (Ictalurus punctatus) has bluish gray to silvery sides, usually with dark spots on smaller individuals. The tail has a deep fork. The anal fin is shorter and more rounded than that of a blue cat.

Channel catfish range.

why "stinkbaits" are so popular. It is true that channels and, to a lesser extent, blues, consume foods of this type. But live foods, such as fish, clams, snails, crayfish and aquatic insect larvae, comprise most of their diet. In fact, flatheads rarely eat dead or rotting food.

Catfish do some feeding during the day, but they feed more heavily at night, especially in waters that are relatively clear.

Compared to most freshwater gamefish, catfish have poor eyesight. But their barbels have a good supply of taste buds, enabling them to find food in muddy water or after dark.

Channel cats have been known to live up to 40 years but, compared to blues and flatheads, they grow slowly. It takes 9 to 15 years for a channel cat to reach 5

pounds. Blues and flatheads, on the other hand, may reach weights of 20 to 30 pounds in only 10 years. It is not known how long blues and flatheads live, but their life span is surely in excess of 20 years.

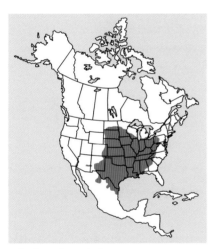

Flathead catfish range.

Blue catfish range.

The flathead catfish (Pylodictis olivaris) has a flattened forehead; very small eyes; mottled, brownish yellow sides; a squarish tail and a lower jaw that protrudes beyond the upper.

The blue catfish (Ictalurus furcatus) looks much like the channel cat. It has a deeply forked tail, but the sides have no spots and the anal fin is longer and straighter.

Key Locations for Catfish...

In Rivers

Early Spring through Spawning:
- Shallow backwaters where catfish can find undercuts and holes in the bank to serve as spawning sites
- Cavities in rocky bluffs
- Crevices in riprap banks

Summer through Mid-Fall:
- Running sloughs that are fed by water from the main channel
- Riprap banks with a slow current
- Tailwaters below dams, where catfish collect because of the concentration of forage fish

Slack-water areas of tailwaters

- Outside bends, where the current has carved a deep hole, hold cats most of the year
- Deep pools and the riffles just above them (smaller rivers)
- Deep holes downstream of tributaries
- Deep holes below wingdams

Late Fall and Winter:
- Certain deep holes in the river channel are traditional wintering sites, drawing thousands of catfish each year

Washout hole below wingdam

In Man-Made Lakes

Early Spring through Spawning:
- Timbered flats leading into shallow creek arms (pre-spawn)
- Shallow creek arms, especially those that are brushy or have cavities of some type in the bank to serve as nesting sites
- Wooded, brushy humps in creek arms

Summer through Mid-Fall:
- Main-lake points, particularly those that have standing timber and are near the mouths of spawning creeks
- Flooded stock ponds or old lake basins
- The old river channel and deeper creek channels
- Suspended in open water
- Flooded roadbeds
- Submerged humps, particularly those near the old river channel
- Saddles between submerged humps or between a hump and a shoreline point
- Timbered flats, especially those near deep water

Timbered flats along the old river channel

Late Fall and Winter:
- Deep holes and outside bends in the old river channel and in major creek channels
- Deep flooded lake basins

Fishing for Catfish

Serious catfish anglers rely almost exclusively on natural or prepared baits including but not limited to the following: congealed chicken blood, chicken livers, chunks of soap, animal entrails, clam meat (fresh or rotten), frogs, catalpa worms, nightcrawlers, mice, crayfish, Limburger cheese, doughballs, stinkbait, and live or dead fish. For large cats, anglers commonly use baitfish weighing 1 to 2 pounds.

Flatheads are most likely to take live baitfish; channels, dead or prepared baits. Blues will take either and so (at times) will channels and flatheads.

Because catfish commonly hang around logs and other obstructions, you need heavy tackle to pull them away from the cover before they can hang you up. Heavy tackle is also needed to cast the big sinkers and baits.

Although catfishing is best at night, you can often catch cats during the day, especially in low-clarity waters. Rising water also seems to trigger a daytime bite.

As a rule, cats bite best in summer, when the water temperature is 70°F or higher. But anglers seeking trophy blues are finding that they bite well in winter and spring as well.

Recommended Tackle

For channel cats on an unobstructed bottom, you can get by with medium-heavy-power spinning gear with 10- to 14-pound mono. For blues or flatheads in heavy cover, use a heavy baitcasting outfit with 30- to 50-pound superline.

Still-Fishing

Most catfish anglers take advantage of the fish's strong sense of smell by still-fishing with natural or prepared baits and letting the scent draw cats.

The most common still-fishing technique is slip-sinker fishing. With a slip-sinker rig, a catfish can move off with your bait without feeling resistance.

Most anglers use a slip-sinker rig with an 18- to 24-inch leader; a barrel swivel connects the leader to the line and serves as a sinker stop.

When you're fishing in snaggy cover, however, you may want to eliminate the swivel and let the sinker slide all the way down to your hook. This way, you can keep the bait snubbed closely to the hook so it can't swim around and tangle in the cover.

A slip-sinker rig may not be necessary when you're fishing for big cats. A little resistance doesn't bother them, so you can affix the sinker to the line.

When catfish are suspended, try a slip-float rig (below). If you can see the fish on your depth finder, set the float to keep the bait at precisely the same depth. A slip-float rig is also a good choice when catfish are scattered over a large flat with a consistent depth. Simply cast the rig upwind and let it drift across the flat.

When still-fishing for channel cats, you can greatly boost your odds by chumming. Before fishing your spot, spread fermented corn, wheat or milo over the area, then come back at least an hour later and fish right in the area you chummed.

Make a slip-sinker rig by sliding a ¹/₂- to 3-ounce egg sinker onto your line and then attaching a barrel swivel, leader and hook suited to your bait.

Popular Catfish Baits

(1) Live baitfish, such as a sucker or sunfish hooked through the lips or the back; (2) cut sucker, shad or herring: (3) gob of crawlers; (4) chicken liver; (5) ball of stinkbait.

Make a slip-float rig by tying a bobber stop onto the line and then sliding on a bead and a cylinder float. Tie on a barrel swivel and add a leader, sinker and hook.

Drift-Fishing

Drift-fishing with several rods is even more effective than slip-float fishing when catfish are scattered over large flats. It also works well for cats around boulders, logs or other obstructions in rivers.

Rig each rod with a 1- to 2-ounce sinker and a live baitfish or a piece of cut bait on a size 3/0 to 6/0 hook, and set the rod so the bait is just off bottom.

To drift-fish a large flat, motor to the upwind side and let the wind push you over it. Make parallel drifts until the entire flat has been covered. If necessary, use a sea anchor to slow your drift.

The same basic technique works well for drift-fishing in a river. Catfish often hold in eddies downstream of boulders and other large obstructions, and drifting your bait

through these areas can be highly effective. Holding the rod in your hand, lower the bait to the bottom and keep your line as vertical as possible as you drift. Keep adjusting your depth as the bottom changes.

Should you find an eddy or hole that is holding good numbers of catfish, anchor just upstream of the spot and try still-fishing.

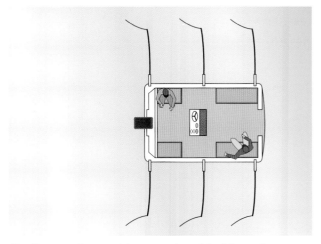

Outfit your boat with several rod holders along each gunwale and place an 8- to 9-foot rod in each. With the rods perpendicular to the gunwales, you can cover a 20- to 25-foot swath of water.

Drift-fish an eddy below a boulder or a deep slot by lowering your bait to the bottom and then reeling it up a few inches. Use a trolling motor to adjust your drift speed.

Experiment with jug lines of different lengths; mark the length of the line on each jug. Then, it will be easy to determine the most productive depths when you retrieve the jugs.

Jug Fishing

Jug fishing is one of the most effective ways to catch cats. Not only does it enable you to cover a wide expanse of water, it works well for cats that are suspended.

Simply attach a line to a sealed jug, add a pinch-on or twist-on sinker, tie on a hook and add your favorite bait. Then let the rig drift through a likely catfish spot.

Some fishermen use a dozen jugs or more.

When you're using small baits and there is little chance of catching big cats, one-quart jugs are adequate. But when you're using big baitfish or fishing for giant cats, use two-quart to one-gallon jugs. A big catfish can submerge a one-quart jug and snag up your line. For maximum visibility, your jugs should be white or fluorescent orange.

You can drift along with the jugs and keep an eye on them, or you can release them on the upwind side of a lake and pick them up later on the downwind side.

When you see a jug bobbing, dipping under or moving against the wind, a cat has taken the bait. There is no need to set the hook; the fish hooks itself when it tries to pull the jug under.

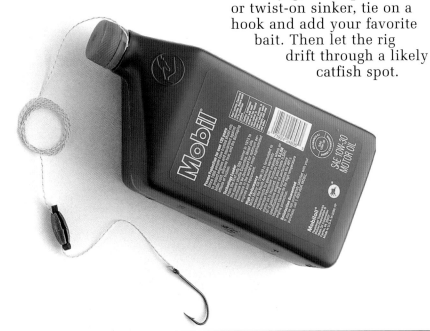

Make a jug-fishing rig by tying the line to the handle or neck. Then add a 1- to 3-ounce sinker and tie on a size 1/0 to 6/0 hook. If desired, use several hooks attached by short leaders to loops in the line.

SUNFISH

Catching sunfish is not much of a challenge; they abound in practically any body of water well-suited to largemouth bass. But catching big sunfish is another matter. In most waters, a 1-pound-plus sunfish is as hard to come by as a trophy bass, walleye or pike.

There are more than a dozen species of sunfish in North America, with the largest (and most popular) being the bluegill (*Lepomis macrochirus*) and the redear sunfish (*Lepomis microlophus*), also known as the shellcracker. Many anglers, particularly those in the South, don't even attempt to distinguish the different species, lumping them all together as bream, or brim.

A great deal of hybridization occurs among the sunfish species. In some waters, cross-breeding is so common that it's difficult to know what you are catching.

Sunfish Facts

Sunfish spawn in spring, when the water temperature is in the upper 60s. The male selects a spawning site, usually at a depth of 3 feet or less on a sandy or gravelly bottom protected from the wind. He sweeps away the silt with his tail, making a light-colored depression. After the female

deposits her eggs, the male aggressively guards the nest until the fry disperse.

The reproductive potential of sunfish is extremely high, with a single female sometimes depositing more than 200,000 eggs. Spawning may occur at monthly intervals over the summer, usually around the full moon. Unless there is

Bluegill range.

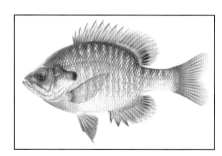

Bluegills have a light blue edge on the gill cover. The "ear" is pure black and there is a black blotch at the rear of the dorsal fin. The sides are brownish-gold with a purple sheen. The male's breast is copper colored; the female's, yellowish.

enough predation to thin the sunfish crop, stunting is likely. As a result, waters with low sunfish populations generally produce the largest fish.

Sunfish feed mainly on small crustaceans and mollusks, fish fry and aquatic insects. They eat more larval insects than adults, although there are times when bluegills take large numbers of adult insects off the surface. Redears seldom feed on the surface; they commonly pick up invertebrates, particularly snails, off the bottom, explaining why they're called shellcrackers.

Practically any warm, shallow, weedy waters will support sunfish. They abound in small, shallow lakes, in protected bays of larger lakes and in slow-moving reaches or backwater areas of rivers and streams. They prefer water temperatures in the mid to upper 70s.

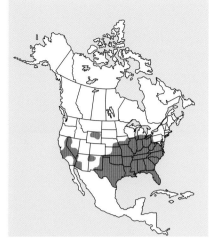

Redear sunfish range.

Redear sunfish get their name from the reddish margin around the otherwise black ear. The sides are light greenish or goldish with scattered reddish flecks.

Of all the freshwater gamefish, sunfish are the most willing biters. And when you hook one on light tackle, it gives you a good tussle for its size. But there is another important reason for the tremendous popularity of sunfish – they're tops on the dinner table. They have firm, white, flaky, sweet-tasting meat.

Sunfish may live up to 10 years, but their usual life span is 5 years or less. Their growth rate is highly variable, depending mainly on population density.

Key Sunfish Locations...

In Natural Lakes
Early Spring through Spawning:
- Shallow, mud-bottomed bays and channels that warm earlier than the main lake (pre-spawn)
- Shallow bays and harbors with a sandy or gravelly bottom (spawning)
- Sheltered sandy or gravelly shorelines (spawning)
- Gradually sloping points with emergent weeds (spawning)

Summer through Mid-Fall:
- Points along weedlines
- Underwater lips of shoreline points
- Weedy humps
- Around deep-water docks
- In deep weed beds

Late Fall and Winter:
- Shallow bays (early winter)
- Deep holes in shallow bays or shallow parts of the main lake
- Inside turns along weedlines

In Man-Made Lakes
Early Spring through Spawning:
- Back ends of creek arms
- Marinas
- Slow-tapering points in creek arms
- Shallow, brushy flats along creek channels
- Main-lake coves with woody cover

Summer through Mid-Fall:
- Main-lake humps
- Extended lips off points in main lake and deep creek arms
- Along the edges of creek channels and the old river channel
- Around intersections of creek channels and the old river channel
- Edges of old roadbeds

Late Fall and Winter:
- In old stock ponds or lake basins
- Deep holes at mouths of creek arms
- Deep sections of creek channels and old river channel

In Rivers
Early Spring through Spawning:
- Shallow, weedy backwaters
- In stands of emergent vegetation along shorelines with practically no current

Summer through Mid-Fall:
- In weedy or woody cover along the edge of the main channel (smaller rivers)
- Deep backwaters with weedy or woody cover
- Along riprap banks with slow-moving water
- Around piers and breakwaters
- Around weedy wingdams with slow current

Late Fall and Winter:
- Deep, slack-water holes in main channel (smaller rivers)
- Shallow backwaters (early and late winter)
- Deep holes in backwaters (midwinter)

Use an extra-long-shank hook, about size 8, when fishing with live bait. The long shank makes it easy to unhook the fish should it swallow the bait.

Recommended Tackle

A light spinning rod and a small reel spooled with 4-pound mono make a good all-around sunfish outfit. Don't use a long, whippy ultralight rod, however, because you'll have trouble getting solid hooksets.

For dabbling in heavy cover, use a 10- to 14-foot extension pole or cane pole with 8- to 12-pound mono.

Fishing for Sunfish

The key to catching sunfish is location. You can find the small ones in harbors, around docks and in most any kind of shallow, weedy cover. But once

An extension pole enables you to place your bait in a small pocket in dense cover. You would have little chance of hitting the pocket by casting and, even if you did, the splash would spook the fish.

spawning is completed, the big ones head for deeper water. It's not unusual to catch them by accident on deep structure while fishing for bass or walleyes. A good depth finder makes the job of locating them a lot easier.

Once you find the fish, catching them shouldn't be much of a problem. A worm on a plain hook is usually all that's needed, but anglers use a variety of small baits and lures (right).

Live bait is normally fished beneath a small float weighted with enough split shot to keep it just above water. If you're fishing in water more than 8 feet deep, use a slip-bobber rig or just a plain hook and a split shot.

Remember that sunfish are not always on the bottom. Fish in 25 feet of water, for instance, may suspend as much as 10 feet off the bottom, so you'll have to set your float accordingly.

When sunfish are in shallow water, they're easy to catch on a fly rod. All sunfish species will hit small nymphs and wet flies, and bluegills don't hesitate to take tiny poppers and sponge bugs.

Sunfish Baits & Lures

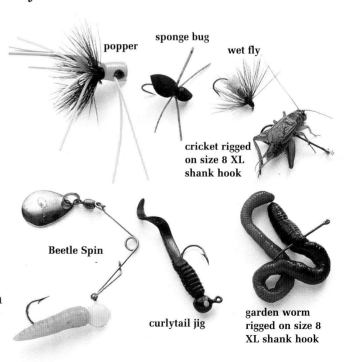

popper

sponge bug

wet fly

cricket rigged on size 8 XL shank hook

Beetle Spin

curlytail jig

garden worm rigged on size 8 XL shank hook

Ice-Fishing baits

ant with mousie

horizontal jig
with waxworm

Teardrop with
goldenrod grub

Fat Boy with
Eurolarvae

Look for goldenrod grubs
in the pods of goldenrod
plants.

Ice Fishing

On many northern waters, more sunfish are taken through the ice than during the open-water season.

By far the most effective ice-fishing method is jigging with a small teardrop or ice fly tipped with a grub, such as a waxworm or maggot. Use a graphite rod with an extremely light tip (right) and spool up with 2- to 4-pound mono. You'll be able to detect the lightest sunfish nibble.

Sunfish bite best just after freeze up. Look for them in the same shallow bays where you found them in spring. They move to deeper water in midwinter and don't bite as well. They return to the shallows in late winter and fishing picks up again.

Select an ice-fishing rod with an extremely flexible tip (top). An ordinary rod won't flex enough to signal a bite, so you'll have to add a spring bobber (bottom).

Jigging your bait rapidly and then letting it rest is a deadly sunfish method – in winter and summer.

CRAPPIES

outdoor press is now devoting more space to crappie fishing and tournament crappie fishing is on the increase.

Crappie Facts

Black crappies *(Pomoxis nigromaculatus)* and white crappies *(Pomoxis annularis)* are often found in the same lakes and streams, but whites can tolerate murkier water. Blacks are most numerous in the North; whites, in the South. Both species prefer a water temperature in the 70- to 75°F range, although they

Black crappie range.

Black crappies have 7 or 8 spines on the dorsal fin and are deeper-bodied than whites. Black speckles on the silvery green sides explain why crappies (black and white) are often called "specks."

The phrase "here today, gone tomorrow," must have been coined by a crappie fisherman. Crappies are known for their nomadic habits, and finding a consistent locational pattern is nearly impossible, especially in summer. This explains why most crappie fishing is

done in spring, when the fish move into the shallows to feed and, later, spawn. You can generally find them in the same springtime locations year after year.

Despite the difficulty of staying on the fish, the popularity of crappie fishing has exploded in recent years. The

can survive at temperatures in the upper 80s.

Compared to most other gamefish, crappies can tolerate lower levels of dissolved oxygen. Consequently, they are usually one of the most common gamefish in lakes that periodically freeze out.

Crappies spawn in spring, usually at water temperatures in the low 60s. They nest on a sandy or gravelly bottom, usually with brush or emergent vegetation for cover. In the North, stands of dead bulrushes from the previous year are key spawning sites. The nests are not as apparent as those of sunfish, because the bottom is not swept as clean. After spawning has been completed, the male remains to guard the eggs and newly hatched fry.

At spawning time, male crappies turn considerably darker than the females and are sometimes nearly black. The males are much more

White crappie range.

aggressive and easier to catch than the females.

The main reason crappies are so difficult to locate is that they spend a good deal of their time feeding on suspended plankton in open water. Other important foods include small fish and aquatic insect larvae.

Crappies are willing biters but, compared to sunfish, are

White crappies have 5 or 6 spines on the dorsal fin and the forehead has a deeper depression than that of the black crappie. The sides normally have 7 to 9 vertical bars.

not strong fighters. They have white meat with a mild flavor, but it is softer than that of sunfish.

Black crappies have a longer life span than whites, with some individuals surviving to an age of 10. But the usual life span for both species is 5 or 6. In the North, a 1-pound crappie is usually 7 or 8 years old; in the South, only about 5.

Key Locations for Crappies...

In Natural Lakes
Early Spring:
- Shallow mud-bottom bays, dead-end channels and harbors
- Channels between lakes

Spring (spawning):
- Sheltered bays and shorelines with a firm bottom and emergent weeds
- Shallow humps with emergent weeds

Summer and Early Fall:
- Deep rock piles
- Edges of weedy humps
- Irregular weedlines
- Gradually tapering points

Late Fall and Winter:
- Inside turns along deep weedlines
- Deep holes in a shallow basin
- Deep water off ends of points
- Deep flats

In Man-Made Lakes
Early Spring:
- Secondary creek arms
- Marinas
- Shallow coves on main lake
- Breakline near spawning cover
- Standing timber
- Fallen trees and brush piles

Spring (spawning):
- Brushy back ends of creek arms
- Feeder creeks with woody cover
- Marinas

Summer and Early Fall:
- Edges of main river channel
- Edges of creek channels
- Main-lake points

Late Fall and Winter:
- Main river channel
- Deep creek channels
- Deep main-lake coves

In Rivers
Early Spring through Spawning:
- Shallow, dead-end sloughs and other backwaters off the main river
- Fallen trees and brush piles
- Shallow sandbars
- Stump fields
- Boat harbors

Late Spring to Early Fall
- Sloughs with current
- Deep holes in backwaters
- Side channels leading into backwaters
- Deep eddies
- Deep outside bends
- Undercut banks and ledges

Late Fall and Winter:
- Deep holes in backwaters
- Deep eddies in main channel

Fishing for Crappies

Whether you're fishing a shallow bay in early spring, a brush pile at spawning time or a deep hump in mid-summer, you can catch crappies on a small minnow dangling beneath a float. This simple technique accounts for more crappies than all other methods combined.

In spring, when the fish are shallow, you can use a float that clips onto or is pegged to your line. In summer, when the fish may be at depths of 20 feet or more, a slip-bobber works much better.

You can also catch crappies on a variety of small, minnow-imitating lures, the most common being a lead-head jig with a soft-plastic or chenille-and-marabou dressing.

Regardless of what lure or bait you use, depth control is of utmost importance in crappie fishing, because of the fish's habit of suspending in a specific depth zone. Experienced anglers rely heavily on their depth finders, spotting the fish and adjusting their depths accordingly.

Recommended Tackle

A light spinning outfit with 4- to 6-pound mono is ideal for fishing crappies in open water. However, when they're buried in brush or other woody cover, you'll need a heavier spinning outfit with 10-pound mono. This, way, you'll be able to straighten a light-wire hook, should it hang up on a branch.

Small jigs are hard to beat for springtime crappies.

Popular Crappie Baits

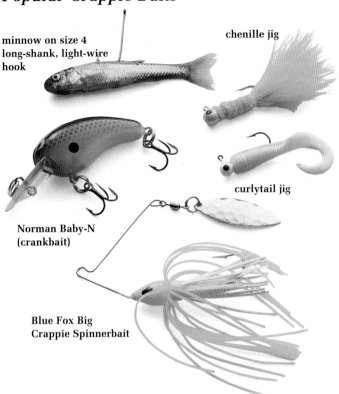

minnow on size 4 long-shank, light-wire hook

chenille jig

curlytail jig

Norman Baby-N (crankbait)

Blue Fox Big Crappie Spinnerbait

Jigs aren't just for open water; you can use them through the ice as well.

When using a small jig or other slow-sinking bait, try the countdown technique. Make a cast, count while the bait sinks, then begin your retrieve. Keep trying different counts until you get a strike, then repeat the same count on subsequent casts.

Fly fishing with small, light-colored streamers and wet flies can be quite effective, but don't bother trying poppers. Crappies are not nearly as surface-oriented as bluegills.

Ice fishermen also depend on their depth finders to locate crappies. After spotting some fish, drop down a minnow on a size 4 hook or a small jigging bait and fish right above the level of the fish.

Crappies move about just as much in winter as they do in summer, so it's important for ice fishermen to be mobile. If you don't catch anything in a few minutes, try another hole.

Ice-Fishing Baits

Jigging Rapala

teardrop tipped with Eurolarvae

Purist (icefly)

Vingla (jigging spoon)

Swedish Pimple tipped with waxworm

Spider-Rigging for Crappies

In the South, where most states allow anglers to use multiple lines, crappie fishermen spider-rig vast expanses of open water to locate schools of suspended crappies.

Although there are times when spider-riggers troll at random, following no distinct structure, they more often follow a breakline. It might be the edge of a creek channel leading into a spawning cove, or it could be a drop-off along a main-lake point.

Start by selecting lures that run at different depths; most anglers use curlytail jigs, hair jigs, jig-spinner combinations or small spinnerbaits (right). Any of these baits can be tipped with small minnows, but it may not be necessary.

For maximum coverage, use the longest rods you have. Ten- to twelve-foot rods are ideal, although some anglers use 16-footers. Be sure the rods have a fast tip; otherwise, the fish won't hook themselves when they strike.

Trolling speed is critical. Crappies seldom strike a fast-moving bait, so it's important to move as slowly as possible, keeping your lines near vertical.

Keep a close eye on your sonar unit to determine if you're on fish. With a wide-angle transducer, you may even be able to see if your lines are tracking at the right depth.

Lures for Spider-Rigging

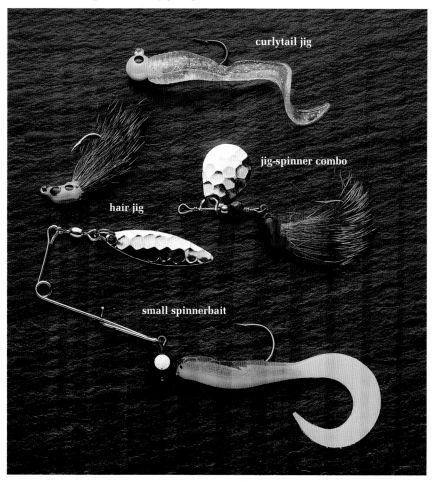

curlytail jig

jig-spinner combo

hair jig

small spinnerbait

Five Crappie-Fishing Tips

Sight-fish for crappies on clear waters during the spawning period. They're easy to see if you wear polarized sunglasses. Use an extension pole; this way, you can dangle a jig in their faces from a distance without spooking them.

Look for male crappies, which are considerably darker than the females at spawning time. Males are far more aggressive than females during the spawning period.

Use a floating "crappie light" when night fishing. The light is directed downward to attract minnows, which, in turn, draw crappies.

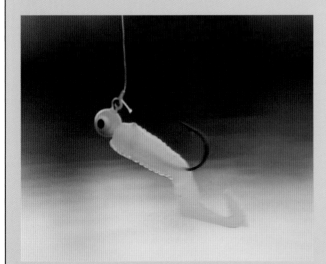

Position your knot so the jig hangs horizontally. If your knot slides to the front of the eye, the jig will hang vertically and will not look natural.

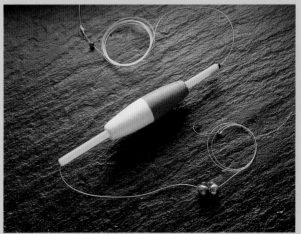

Make a slip-bobber rig by tying a slip-bobber knot on your line and threading on a small bead and a float. Then add a split shot and a hook. Adjust the stop to fish at the desired depth.

YELLOW PERCH

Perca flavescens

When the yellow perch are biting, word travels fast. And if you've ever dined on a plate of fresh perch fillets, you know why. Many fish connoisseurs rate them ahead of walleyes on the table-quality scale.

Yellow perch are close relatives of walleyes and inhabit many of the same waters. They abound in large, clear northern lakes with clean, sandy bottoms and have been stocked extensively throughout the country.

Perch, like walleyes, are considered coolwater fish. Their preferred temperature range is 65 to 72°F, but they continue to feed aggressively at much lower water temperatures and are very popular among ice anglers.

Spawning takes place in early spring at water temperatures in the mid-40s. Gelatinous strands of eggs are deposited on sticks, rocks, weeds and other debris and, when conditions are right for a successful hatch, the shallows are soon teeming with huge numbers of young perch.

Yellow perch eat small fish, fish eggs, larval aquatic insects, snails and crustaceans, especially crayfish and scuds. Perch do most of their feeding near the

Yellow perch have yellowish sides with 6 to 9 dark, vertical bars. The lower fins often have an orange tinge, particularly in spawning males.

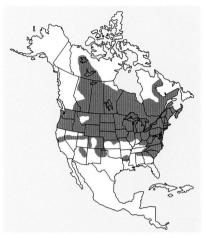

Yellow perch range

A plain jig or a jig and minnow probably account for more perch than any other bait. Simply bounce it slowly along the bottom and set the hook whenever you feel a tap or the bait suddenly feels lighter.

Popular Perch Baits

small minnow
on size 4 hook

in-line
spinner

marabou jig

piece of nightcrawler
on size 4 hook

Most yellow perch fishermen rely on live bait fished on either a split-shot or slip-sinker rig with a size 4 to 6 hook, or tipped on a jig or spinner. It's possible, however, to take perch on small artificials, such as marabou jigs and in-line spinners.

Interest in ice fishing for yellow perch has exploded in recent years. Anglers use their electronics to pinpoint schools of perch on mid-lake structure and then jig for them using a $2\frac{1}{2}$- to 3-foot graphite jigging rod, 4-pound mono and a small spoon or lead-head jig tipped with live bait. The fastest action is usually in late winter, when meltwater starts running down the holes.

bottom and commonly root in the mud for the larvae of mayflies and other insects.

In many small lakes, perch never reach a size large enough to interest fishermen. Your best bets for "jumbo" perch (those weighing $\frac{3}{4}$ pound or more) are large, shallow, sandy natural lakes with minimal weed growth.

A light spinning outfit with 4- to 6-pound mono is ideal for yellow perch. The fish are not powerful fighters, and the light outfit makes it easy to cast lightweight baits.

Ice-Fishing Baits

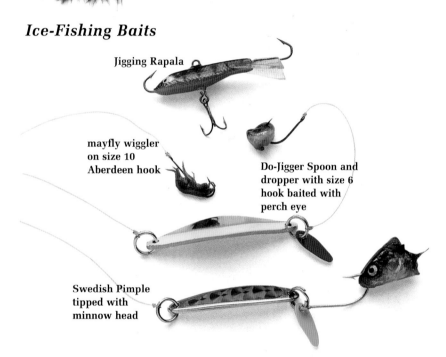

Jigging Rapala

mayfly wiggler
on size 10
Aberdeen hook

Do-Jigger Spoon and dropper with size 6 hook baited with perch eye

Swedish Pimple
tipped with
minnow head

Tips for Catching Perch

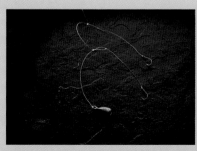

A tandem-hook rig allows you to catch perch two at a time. Tie a pair of double-surgeon's loops (p.63) in your line, attach leaders and hooks and add a bell sinker.

Use a "hanger rig,"consisting of a steel rod with a hook at the end, to get down quickly and stir up the bottom. The disturbance attracts perch.

Modify a jigging spoon by adding a mono dropper and size 6 hook. Bait up with a minnow head, perch eye or waxworm. The spoon gets the bait down fast and adds attraction.

NORTHERN PIKE & MUSKELLUNGE

Esox lucius & Esox masquinongy

When you catch a glimpse of a huge pike or muskie inches behind your lure, your knees are bound to get a little shaky. And when the fish grabs your bait and makes a screeching run toward the weeds, you'd better hope you spooled on heavy enough line and tied good knots.

Besides the northern pike and muskie, the pike family also includes the chain pickerel, which seldom exceeds 5 pounds, and the grass and redfin pickerel, which rarely reach 1 pound.

Pike & Muskie Facts

Although pike and muskies are both found in weedy portions of natural lakes and in slow-moving, weedy rivers, muskies seldom thrive in waters with an abundance of pike. The pike hatch earlier in the season and, because they are larger, prey upon the newly hatched muskies.

Both species are classified as coolwater fish, preferring water in the mid-60s to low 70s. But once pike reach a length of about 30 inches, they favor water that is considerably cooler, about 50 to 55°F.

Pike spawn in early spring, usually when the water reaches the low to mid 40s. Spawning sites include tributary streams, connecting marshes and shallow, weedy bays. Muskies spawn several weeks later, as water temperatures reach the upper 40s to upper 50s. They scatter their eggs in weedy bays, but may also spawn on weedy flats in the main lake. Neither species make any attempt to guard the eggs or young.

Because of the great difference in spawning time, hybridization between pike and muskies rarely takes place in nature. But hybrids, called tiger muskies, are commonly raised in hatcheries and have been stocked in many parts of the country. Tiger muskies are more aggressive than purebred muskies, so they're easier to catch, but they don't grow quite as large.

The genetic makeup of muskies is quite variable. There are three distinct

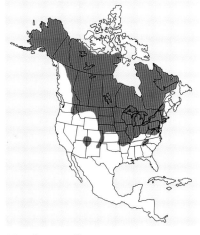

Northern pike range.

Muskie range.

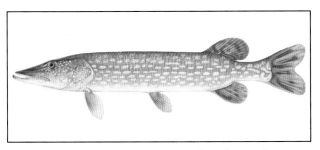

Northern pike have dark greenish sides with rows of oval-shaped, cream-colored spots. The tail has large dark spots and the lobes are rounded.

Muskies have dark spots or bars on light greenish to silvery sides. Or they may be unspotted. The tail has smaller spots, or no spots, and sharper lobes.

Muskies lurk in heavy cover, waiting for unsuspecting baitfish.

attacking quickly. Pike are primarily daytime feeders; muskies, especially those in clear lakes, also feed at night.

All members of the pike family have long, sharp teeth with a razor-like edge (below) that can easily cut your line. Contrary to popular belief, they do not lose their teeth in summer. Rather, their teeth are continually being broken off and replaced by new ones.

In warmwater lakes and streams, pike seldom live longer than 6 years, but muskies may live up to 12. Both species have a much longer life span in colder waters, with pike living as long as 25 years; muskies, 30. Muskies grow much faster than pike. A 20-pound pike is likely to be more than 20 years old; a muskie of the same size, only 10.

color phases: barred, spotted and clear. But these varieties are not considered true subspecies. Because of widespread muskie stocking, any of these color phases may be found throughout the muskie's range.

Fish make up most of the diet of both species, but they also eat frogs, mice, ducklings and even muskrats. Pike, however, are more aggressive feeders, striking most anything that comes into view. Muskies size up their prey more carefully, lying dormant until the moment is right, then

Tiger muskies have light sides with dark, narrow, vertical bars, which are often broken into spots. The lobes of the tail are rounder than a muskie's.

Pike and muskies have large teeth with very sharp edges (inset).

Key Locations for Pike and Muskie...

In Shallow Natural Lakes

Early Spring through Spawning:
- Marshes connected to the main lake

Spawning bay

- Shallow, weedy bays

Late Spring through Early Summer:
- Weedlines and weedy humps and points, particularly those near spawning bays
- Shallow gravel or rock bars

Mid-Summer through Early Fall:
- Beds of lily pads or other float-ing-leaved vegetation that keeps the water slightly cooler
- Bars, points and flats with a healthy growth of submerged weeds, particularly cabbage

Cabbage bed

- Edges of deep bulrush beds
- Weedy saddles connecting two islands or a point and an island
- Inflowing springs (pike)

Late Fall and Winter:
- Deep, rocky humps
- Deep holes surrounded by shal-low water (in lakes that do not have low oxygen levels)

In Deep Natural Lakes

Early Spring through Spawning:
- Shallow, mud-bottomed bays attract pike soon after ice out, and muskies a few weeks later

Late Spring through Early Summer:
- Shallow flats just outside of spawning bays, particularly those

Rocky flat outside of spawning bay

with weedy or rocky cover
- Channels leading from the spawning bay to the main lake

Mid-Summer through Early Fall:
- Mouths of good-sized inlet streams (these areas hold pike and muskies from late spring through fall)
- Rocky reefs below the thermo-cline (pike)
- Shallow rocky reefs (muskie)
- Deep narrows that have moving water on windy days
- Clusters of islands that have extended lips with submerged weed beds
- Weedy or rocky points that slope gradually into deep water

Late Fall:
- Gravelly shoals and points that serve as spawning areas for cis-coes (when the water tempera-ture drops to the mid-40s)
- Rocky points and humps that slope sharply into deep water

Winter:
- Shallow bays

In Rivers

Early Spring through Spawning:
- Shallow backwater lakes (big rivers)
- Seasonally flooded sloughs (smaller rivers)

Late Spring through Early Summer:
- Tailwaters of dams
- Deep, weedy backwaters and side channels

Mid-Summer through Mid-Fall:
- Good-sized eddies that form below islands, points or sand bars
- Current breaks, where there is a distinct line between fast and slow water
- Spring holes (pike)
- Mouths of coldwater streams (pike)

Cold tributary flowing into river

Late Fall and Winter:
- Shallow backwater areas (through early winter)
- Deep holes in backwaters (late winter)
- Impoundments above low-head dams (smaller rivers)

Year-Round Locations (smaller rivers):
- Deep pools with light current
- Deep oxbow lakes off main river

Oxbow lake

Fishing Techniques

Pike and muskies consume a wide variety of foods, so it's not surprising that they'll strike most any kind of bait. As a rule, size and action of the bait are a lot more important than color.

Experienced pike and muskie anglers know that big baits catch big fish, so they do not hesitate to use lures measuring nearly a foot long. Of course, you'll need stout tackle to cast baits this size and to drive the hooks into the fishes' bony mouths.

Muskies, especially those in heavily fished waters, are notorious followers. They will pursue the bait right up to the boat and then turn away at the last instant. But you can often make them strike by reeling the bait to within a foot of the rod tip, then pushing the tip as far into the water as you can and making large figure-eights. This tactic is seldom necessary with pike.

To preserve quality pike and muskie fishing, anglers must learn to practice catch-and-release. Otherwise, the big fish are quickly removed. Always carry jaw spreaders and heavy longnose pliers. If possible, remove the hooks while the fish is still in the water.

Recommended Tackle

A medium-heavy-power bait-casting outfit with 12- to 20-pound mono or superline is adequate for the majority of pike and muskie fishing. For trophy-caliber fish, however, you'll need a heavy-power outfit with 25- to 50-pound line. Always use a steel leader for pike and muskie fishing.

Spinnerbaits work well in heavy cover. Because of the safety-pin design, the hook is protected.

Fishing with Spinnerbaits & Bucktails

When pike or muskies are in weedy cover, a spinnerbait is hard to beat. You can retrieve it over a weedy flat, keeping it just above the weed tops or allowing the blade to slightly "bulge" the surface. You can also let it helicopter into any holes in the weeds, or fish it on the bottom with a jigging motion. When the fish are suspended, try counting a spinnerbait down to their level.

Spinnerbaits come in single- and tandem-blade models. Singles are best for helicoptering, but tandems give off more vibration, an advantage for fishing in murky water or at night.

Bucktails are large in-line spinners with dressings of natural or synthetic hair. They can be fished in sparse weeds but, because they have open hooks, are not a good choice in dense vegetation. The combination of the billowing hair, thumping blade and good hooking performance makes bucktails a favorite of many veteran pike and muskie anglers.

Buchertail (bucktail spinner)

M&G Musky Tandem Spinnerbait

Topwaters

If you've ever seen a pike or muskie attack a duckling, frog or mouse, you know they're accustomed to grabbing food on the surface. Yet, for some reason, topwater fishing never enters the minds of many pike and muskie anglers.

There are times, however, when topwaters work even better than the standard subsurface fare. When the fish are buried in dense weeds, for instance, you can often draw them out with a topwater. And the bait won't foul as much as a subsurface offering.

Muskie fanatics know that topwaters are deadly for night fishing. The more noise and splash the lure produces, the better.

Topwaters are not a good choice in cool water. When the water temperature is below 60°F, choose a subsurface bait.

The topwaters used for pike and muskie fishing are similar to those used for bass fishing, but are considerably larger.

Propbaits have a propeller on the front or back end, or both. On some baits, the whole head or tail serves as a propeller. A slow, steady retrieve usually works best.

Buzzbaits come in safety-pin and in-line models. You can retrieve them rapidly, so they're a good choice when you're trying to locate fish.

Crawlers, with their cupped face or "arms," swim with a wide wobble and make a loud gurgling sound. They're most effective with a slow, straight retrieve.

Stickbaits are weighted in the tail, so they have a highly erratic, side-to-side motion when retrieved with a series of sharp downward jerks. Although their action is attractive to pike and muskies, the fish may have a hard time zeroing in on the darting bait.

Work a stickbait with sharp downward jerks.

Poe's Giant Jackpot (stickbait)

Gooch's Tallywacker (propbait)

Creeper (crawler)

Buchertail Super Buzz

Fishing with Subsurface Plugs

With fish being such an important food for pike and muskies, the effectiveness of subsurface plugs should come as no surprise.

Because of their open hooks, these baits are used mainly in sparse cover or open water. If you're fishing in weeds, select a bait that runs just above the weed tops. In open water, the bait should periodically contact the bottom.

Pike and muskie anglers rely mainly on three kinds of subsurface plugs. Minnowbaits, with their narrow lip and slim body, have a tight, natural-looking wobble. Crankbaits have a broader lip or flattened head that produces a wider wobble. Vibrating plugs, with the attachment eye on the flattened back, have the fastest, tightest wiggle.

The best plugs have hooks anchored to an internal wire, rather than attached with screw eyes that a big fish could pull out.

Any of these plugs can be fished by casting or trolling. Although you can catch fish with a steady retrieve, a stop-and-go presentation usually draws more strikes.

Use a thin, braided-wire leader with a round-nosed snap for attaching subsurface plugs. A heavy wire leader would restrict the plug's side-to-side action.

Bomber Magnum Long-A (minnowbait)

Bill Lewis Super-Trap (vibrating plug)

Bagley DB06 (crankbait)

Jerkbait Fishing

The erratic, struggling-baitfish action of these big wooden plugs has a special appeal to pike and muskies.

The term, "jerkbait," is somewhat of a misnomer, because the baits are retrieved with a series of smooth, downward strokes, rather than sharp jerks. Jerkbaits have no action other than that which the angler provides.

Use a short, stiff rod for jerkbait fishing. If you use a long rod, the tip will hit the water on the down-ward stroke. Attach the bait with a stiff wire leader.

There are dozens of different styles of jerk-baits, but they fall into two categories:

Divers dart downward when you jerk; *gliders* dart from side to side. Divers generally run deeper than gliders, but both types of baits can be doctored for extra depth by adding lead weights (internal or external) or wrapping solder around the hooks.

Spoon Fishing

Spoons are great for beginners because it's nearly impossible to fish them the wrong way. You can use a fast, slow or stop-and-go retrieve, jig them in deep water and even skitter them across the surface.

But spoons aren't just for amateurs; you'll find a good selection in the tackle box of practically every serious pike and muskie angler.

Thick-metal spoons are best for casting, but thinner ones have a wider wobble and are ideal for trolling. In heavy cover, use a weedless spoon. Attach your spoon to a braided-wire leader.

Fudally Reef Hawg (glider)

Suick (diver)

Windels Hunter (diver)

Bagley B-Flat (glider)

Eppinger Dardevle

Johnson Silver Minnow with curlytail

Jig Fishing

Jig fishing does not enjoy widespread popularity in pike-muskie circles, but when fishing gets tough, it often outshines any other method.

Jigs are a good choice, for instance, when cold water slows pike and muskie activity to the point where they won't chase a bait with a fast or erratic action. They may, however, inhale a jig dropped in front of their nose.

A round-head jig works well in sparse cover or open water but, for fishing in weeds, you'll need a bullet-head with the eye at the front. For fishing over weed tops, try a swimmer-head.

Most pike-muskie jigs come with a soft-plastic dressing, such as a large shad, reaper, creature or curlytail. Some anglers prefer a plain jig head tipped with a big minnow.

Use the lightest jig that you can keep on the bottom. Pike-muskie jigs range from $3/8$ to $3/4$ ounce. Attach your jig to a braided-wire leader.

Fly Fishing

You don't hear much about fly fishing for pike and muskies, but the sport is growing in popularity. And those who go about it the right way know just how effective it can be.

Fly fishing works well any time the fish are in shallow water. Then, they'll take divers, poppers, streamers and frog imitations in sizes 1 to 4/0. Be sure to select a fly with a weedguard if you'll be fishing in heavy cover.

Pike and muskie anglers generally use a 7- to 10-weight fly rod with a floating, weight-forward or bass-bug-taper line. Make sure your leader has a braided-wire shock tippet.

bullet-head jig with reaper

swimmer-head jig with curlytail

round-head jig with shad tail

Dahlberg Mega Diver

Barr's Bouface

streamer

anglers. Oily fish, like smelt and ciscoes, seem to have the most appeal.

Live or dead baitfish can be fished beneath a float or still-fished on the bottom. Live baitfish can also be retrieved slowly on a jig head or slip-sinker rig.

Always rig baitfish on a braided-wire leader with a size 2/0 to 6/0 single hook or a quick-strike rig consisting of a pair of double or treble hooks.

chub

golden shiner

sucker

smelt

Live-Bait Fishing

When pike and muskies are finicky, nothing triggers more strikes than real food.

Although the fish will strike a variety of live baits, including frogs, waterdogs, leeches and nightcrawlers, most anglers opt for large baitfish, such as suckers, chubs and golden shiners.

If you're after good-sized pike or muskies, the problem may be finding baitfish that are large enough. For fish over 10 pounds, you should have lively baitfish at least 8 inches long, and many anglers prefer 10 to 12 inchers.

Dead bait is growing in popularity among pike

Rig a baitfish on a single hook by pushing it in the mouth and out the top of the snout. For float fishing, you can also hook the bait through the back.

Rig a baitfish on a strip-on spinner by pushing the wire through the bait's mouth and out the vent. Then, put the double hook on the wire with the points up.

Rig a baitfish on a quick-strike rig by pushing one hook into the body near the pectoral fin and the other near the dorsal. When a fish strikes, set the hook immediately.

Ice Fishing

Because of their coldwater habits, pike remain active all winter and are a favorite of ice anglers. Muskies, on the other hand, are seldom taken through the ice.

Live or dead baitfish on tip-ups account for the majority of winter pike.

Spool your tip-ups with 25- to 40-pound-test braided Dacron or superline and tie on a braided-wire leader with a size 2/0 to 6/0 single hook, a spinner rig or a quick-strike rig (opposite).

Add enough weight to keep the bait at the desired depth, which may be almost anywhere in the water column. When oxygen levels are low in late winter, it's not uncommon to find pike swimming just under the ice.

Tip-ups enable you to cover a large piece of structure, such as a weed flat or deep hump, much more efficiently than you could with any other method. Scatter your tip-ups at first, then concentrate them after you find the fish.

Popular Rigs for Tip-Up Fishing

Add a small Colorado spinner blade just above a size 2 to 1/0 treble hook, then push one prong of the treble through the back of a lively baitfish. As the baitfish swims about, the blade flashes, drawing extra strikes.

Rig a dead smelt or cisco on a size 3 or 4 Swedish hook. Push the hook into the vent up to the bend, turn the shank up, then push the point of the hook out just behind the head. The bait should ride in a level position.

WALLEYE & SAUGER

Stizostedion vitreum & Stizostedion canadense

Widespread stocking has put walleyes within easy reach of the majority of North American anglers. Saugers are much less common but, where they exist, rival walleyes in popularity.

Walleyes and saugers belong to the perch family. Although walleyes are often called "walleyed pike" and saugers, "sand pike," they are not related to pike or muskies. To further confuse the matter, walleyes in parts of Canada are called "pickerel."

Their firm, white meat, with no fishy taste, explains why walleyes and saugers are among the most popular table fish.

Walleye & Sauger Facts

The eyes of walleyes and saugers differ from those of other freshwater gamefish in that they have a layer of light-reflective pigment, called the *Tapetum lucidum*, in the retina. This layer gives the fish excellent night vision and also causes them to avoid bright sunlight. Saugers have a larger tapetum than walleyes.

It's not unusual for anglers to catch a mixture of walleyes and saugers in the same spot. But saugers, because of their larger tapetum, are usually found in slightly deeper water and are more tolerant of high turbidity.

Considered coolwater fish, walleyes and saugers prefer water temperatures in the 60s to low 70s. Walleyes are most numerous in large, windswept natural lakes of moderate clarity; saugers, in big rivers or reservoirs of low to moderate clarity.

Saugers (left) and walleyes (right) are commonly caught in the same water.

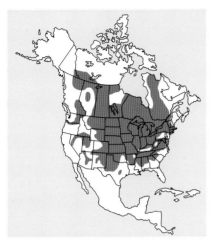

Walleye range.

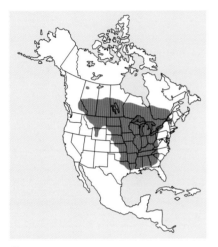

Sauger range.

Walleyes have golden sides and a white belly. The spiny dorsal fin is not spotted, but has a black blotch at the rear base. The lower lobe of the tail has a large, white tip.

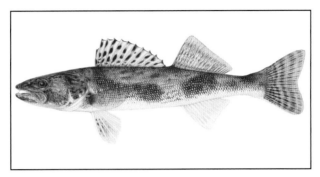

Saugers are grayish to brownish with dark blotches. The dorsal fin has rows of distinct black spots, and the pectoral fins have a dark spot at the base. The lower lobe of the tail may have a thin, white streak.

Walleyes spawn in spring, generally at water temperatures in the upper 40s. Saugers spawn several days later than walleyes. Both species are random spawners, depositing their eggs on clean gravelly or rocky bottoms. Saugers usually spawn a little deeper than walleyes.

The two species sometimes hybridize to produce the *saugeye,* which is intermediate in looks and behavior between the parents.

There are two subspecies of walleyes: the yellow walleye *(Stizostedion vitreum vitreum)* and the blue walleye *(Stizostedion vitreum glaucum).* But the latter, once common in lakes Erie and Ontario, is now believed to be extinct.

Small fish make up most of the diet, but walleyes and saugers also feed on leeches, crayfish, snails, larval aquatic insects and larval salamanders. They feed most heavily in dim-light periods, when their excellent night vision gives them a predatory advantage over most baitfish. Research has shown that rapidly decreasing light levels trigger walleye feeding.

Walleyes and saugers are not flashy fighters; they do not jump or make speedy runs.

Instead, they wage, a strong, determined battle, staying deep and stubbornly shaking their head until they tire.

Walleyes reach a considerably larger size than saugers, mainly because of their longer life span. Walleyes have been known to reach a documented age of 26 years, although they seldom live longer than 10. Saugers may live up to 13 years, but an age of more than 7 is rare.

In the North, walleyes and saugers normally reach a weight of 2 pounds in about 7 years; in the South, they grow to that size in 3 to 4 years. The biggest walleyes come from southern waters, but the largest saugers are found in the North. In the same waters, walleyes usually grow a little faster than saugers.

Saugeyes have a spotted or mottled dorsal fin, but the spots are not as distinct as those of a sauger.

Key Locations for Walleye*...

In Natural Lakes

Early Spring through Spawning:
- Gravel or rubble shorelines that are exposed to the wind
- Inlet streams with rocky or gravelly bottoms
- Shallow, rocky reefs close to shore

Late Spring:
- Gradually tapering points near spawning areas
- Large, shallow flats connected to points

Shallow flat extending off point

- Shallow bays barely connected to the main lake (shield lakes)
- Gravel patches on shallow mud flats
- Shallow, slow-tapering reefs

Summer to Mid-Fall:
- Gradually sloping reefs
- Irregular breaklines with a gradual taper
- Outer tips of long, gradually tapering points
- Mouths of good-sized inlets, particularly in shield lakes
- Breaklines around island clusters
- Sandy, weedy humps in rocky lakes
- Suspended over deep water, particularly in lakes with cisco forage base
- Weedy flats in shallow, fertile lakes

Late Fall and Winter:
- Deep, sharp-sloping reefs
- Irregular breaklines that slope sharply into deep water
- Fringes of bulrush beds on shallow points

In Man-Made Lakes

Early Spring through Spawning:
- Deep pools in tributary streams concentrate the fish before spawning
- The upper end of the old river channel is a pre-spawn staging area (shallow reservoirs)
- Riffles in tributary streams are prime spawning sites
- Gravelly shorelines in the upper end of the reservoir
- Riprap shorelines, such as those along causeways and dam faces

Riprap bank

Late Spring:
- Timbered flats along edges of creek channels
- Shallow, sand-gravel points in creek arms
- Mud flats at upper end of the reservoir

Summer to Mid-Fall:
- Brushy main-lake points near deep water
- Wooded humps near the old river channel
- Timbered flats along the old river channel
- Steep eroded banks with rock slides
- Rocky main-lake points with shallow food shelves

Late Fall and Winter:
- Steep, timbered points and inside turns along the old river channel
- Old ponds and lake basins (shallow reservoirs)
- Deep holes above the dam (mainly in shallow reservoirs)

In Rivers

Early Spring through Spawning:
- Eddies in the vicinity of tailraces hold walleyes prior to and after spawning
- Pools downstream from spawning riffles are pre-spawn staging areas (smaller rivers)
- Riffle areas and rocky shorelines downstream of riffles are prime spawning areas (smaller rivers)
- Flooded willows along the fringes of the main channel draw spawners
- Flooded marshes adjacent to the river draw spawners in high-water years
- Riprap shorelines with small rocks make excellent spawning areas

Late Spring:
- Current-brushed points downstream of spawning areas
- Deep cuts connecting main channel and backwaters
- Deep backwaters
- Deep pools and eddies downstream of spawning areas

Current-brushed point

Summer to Mid-Fall:
- Rocky banks brushed by light current
- Rocky points extending into the river and the eddies formed by them
- Wingdams
- Deep banks with fallen trees
- Upper ends of deep pools (smaller rivers)

Late Fall and Winter:
- Deep holes along outside bends
- Deep eddies and slow-moving slots in tailrace areas

---

* Note: Sauger inhabit many of the same areas as walleye, but are slightly deeper.

A jig tipped with live bait is one of the most consistent walleye and sauger producers.

Recommended Tackle

A medium- to medium-heavy-power spinning outfit with 6- to 8-pound mono is adequate for the majority of walleye and sauger fishing. For trolling applications, however, most anglers prefer medium-heavy-power baitcasting gear spooled with 10- to 14-pound mono or superline. Wire leaders are not necessary for walleye-sauger fishing.

vertically jig it on the bottom as you drift or slowly troll. How much action you impart to the jig depends on the water temperature and the mood of the fish. When the water is below 50°F, or the fish are not aggressive, work the jig with short hops or just drag it along the bottom. When the water is warmer and fish are active, retrieve with bigger hops. Be sure to keep your line taut when the jig is sinking; that's when the fish normally strike. Whenever you feel a light tap or anything out of the ordinary, set the hook.

Walleye & Sauger Techniques

The challenge of catching these finicky biters is exactly what appeals to so many anglers. For consistent success, you must be proficient with a variety of live-bait and artificial-lure presentations.

The techniques used for walleyes and saugers are much the same, with the main difference being that saugers are usually caught in slightly deeper water.

Both species are schooling fish, so once you locate a few, you can bet there are more nearby. Serious walleye and sauger anglers rely heavily on their electronics to find fish and lock in the location of the spot, so they can return at a later time.

Jig Fishing

A lead-head jig is the simplest walleye-sauger bait, yet it is arguably the most consistently effective. It's also one of the least expensive.

Most walleye-sauger jigs weigh from $1/16$ to $1/2$ ounce and have hair, feather or soft-plastic dressings. Jigs can also be tipped with a minnow, leech or piece of nightcrawler.

You can cast a jig and retrieve it along the bottom, or

Fireball Jig with clip-on stinger hook

Fuzz-E-Grub

bullet-head bucktail jig

curlytail jig

jig tipped with Sassy Shad

Slip-Sinker Fishing

Slip-sinker fishing gives you the most natural live-bait presentation possible. And when a fish takes the bait, it feels no resistance; as it swims away, the sinker stays put.

To fish a slip-sinker rig, simply lower it to the bottom, let out just enough line so you can maintain bottom contact, and then slowly troll or drift over good walleye structure. Keep your bail open and hold the line with your finger. This way, you can release the line immediately when you feel a pick-up.

Feed line until the fish stops running, point your rod at the fish, reel rapidly until you feel some weight and then set the hook with a sharp, upward snap of the wrists.

Don't make the mistake of slowly tightening up to see if the fish is still there; that's when it usually drops the bait.

It's important to choose the right type and size of weight. For fishing on a clean bottom, use an egg sinker or walking sinker; in weedy cover, a bullet sinker. You'll need about $1/8$ to $3/16$ ounce of weight for every 10 feet of depth. It takes a little extra weight to maintain bottom contact in windy weather.

Most anglers rig their bait on a plain hook, but some prefer to add a small float to keep the bait off bottom and provide a little color. You can also add a small spinner blade or a colored bead.

Another important issue is leader length. When the fish are hugging bottom, a 3-foot

leader is adequate. But when they're suspended, you'll want a much longer leader and some type of float. Some anglers use leaders more than 10 feet long.

A $6\frac{1}{2}$- to $7\frac{1}{2}$-foot spinning rod with a soft tip and a stiff butt is the best choice for slip-sinker fishing. Then, should you fail to release the line when a fish bites, it won't feel too much resistance and drop the bait. Yet, you'll be able to get a firm hookset.

Be sure to keep your reel filled to within about $1/8$ inch of the rim. If the reel is not full, the line will catch on the lip when a fish runs, causing it to feel resistance and drop the bait. A nick on the lip of the spool can cause the same problem.

A slip-sinker rig allows a walleye to take the bait and swim away without feeling resistance.

Making & Fishing a Slip-Sinker Rig

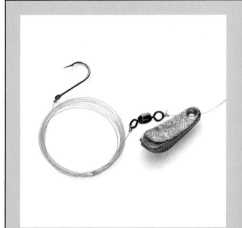

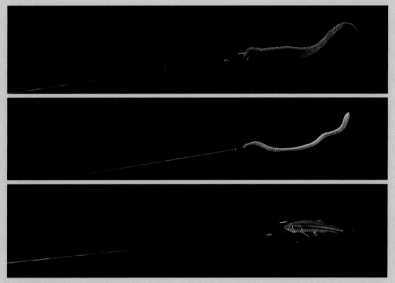

1 *Tie a slip-sinker rig by threading a weight onto 6- to 8-pound mono and then tying on a small barrel swivel. Add a 3- to 5-foot leader of 4- to 6-pound mono and attach a size 4 to 6 short-shank hook.*

2 *Hook a leech (top) just in front of the sucker using a size 6 hook; a nightcrawler (middle), through the head with a size 6 hook; a minnow (bottom), through the lips with a size 4 hook.*

1 *After dropping the rig to the bottom, keep your bail open and hold the line on your finger.*

2 *Release the line immediately when you detect a bite. Sometimes, all you feel is a little extra resistance.*

3 *When the fish stops running, quickly reel up the slack until you feel some weight, then set the hook.*

Optional Slip-Sinker Rigs

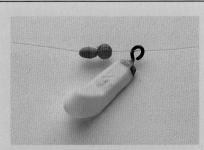

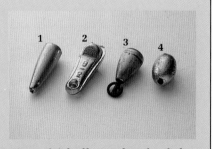

A rig with a rubber stop and bead enables you to change leader length easily. You can buy pre-tied rigs or make your own using a slip-bobber knot (p.64).

*Keep your bait off bottom with **(1)** a floating jig head or **(3)** slip-on float. For extra attraction, add a **(2)** colored bead.*

*Use a **(1)** bullet sinker for fishing in weeds; a **(2)** walking sinker or **(4)** egg sinker on a clean bottom; and a **(3)** clip-on sinker for changing weights quickly.*

Slip-Bobber Fishing

When walleyes are suspended or not feeding aggressively, you can often tease them into biting by using a slip-bobber rig to put the bait right in their face.

The beauty of a slip-bobber rig is that it can be set to fish at any depth, yet will still allow you to reel the bait right up to the rod tip. Otherwise, you would not be able to cast the rig.

A long spinning rod, at least 6½ feet, is recommended for slip-bobber fishing. A long rod helps you get a strong hookset, which may be difficult because the bobber causes your line to form a right angle between you and the fish. When the bobber goes down, be sure to reel in line until you feel weight before setting.

Most slip-bobber fishing is done with leeches, crawlers or minnows, either on a plain hook or a ¹/₁₆- to ¹/₃₂-ounce jig head. For night fishing, use a lighted slip-bobber.

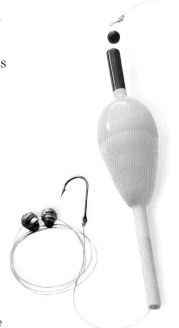

Tie a slip-bobber knot (p.64) on your line, thread on a small bead and the slip-bobber, then tie on a size 4 to 6 hook or a small jig head. Add enough split shot to balance the bobber.

How a Slip-Bobber Works

Cast a slip-bobber rig, then feed line as the bait sinks. The knot moves toward the bobber, which is resting on its side.

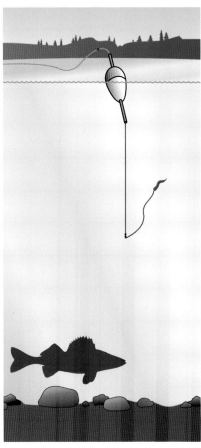

Continue feeding line as the knot approaches the bobber. If you stop feeding line, the rig will pull back toward you.

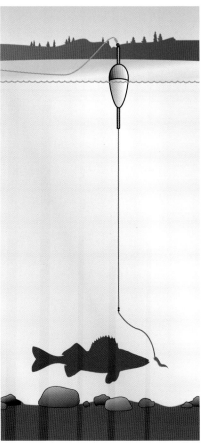

When the knot reaches the bobber, the weight will stand it upright and the bait will be at the desired depth.

Spinner Fishing

It's easy to understand why trolling or drifting with a spinner and live bait is a time-proven method for walleyes and saugers. The vibration and flash from the spinner blade draw attention to the bait.

Spinner rigs are most effective in low-clarity water, where the fish may not spot plain live bait. But many anglers believe that a spinner blade is an asset in any kind of water.

Most spinner rigs are made with a Colorado blade, usually size 2 to 4, because it spins easily even at very slow trolling speeds. In low-clarity waters, use a fluorescent orange, green or chartreuse blade; in clear to moderately clear waters, a silver, gold or brass blade.

A single-hook spinner rig works best for minnows or leeches; a tandem- or triple-hook rig, for nightcrawlers.

A tandem- or triple-hook harness reduces the number of short strikes when you're fishing with a spinner and crawler.

Other Popular Spinner Rigs

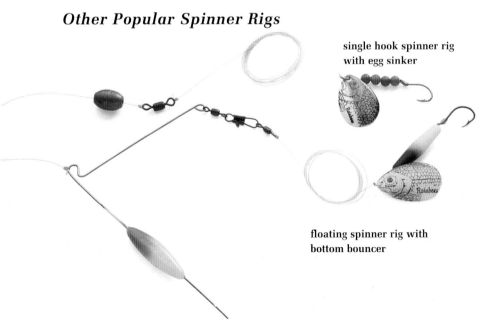

single hook spinner rig with egg sinker

floating spinner rig with bottom bouncer

How much weight you use depends on the water depth and how fast you're trolling or drifting. If you're fishing in 10 feet of water and moving slowly, you need only a ³⁄₈- to ¹⁄₂-ounce sinker. But if you're trolling fast ("power trolling") in 20 feet of water, you may need a 3-ounce weight.

Many spinner addicts prefer bottom-bouncers to ordinary weights, because they keep the bait off bottom and are relatively snagless.

Plug Fishing

Anglers on the pro-walleye circuit will attest to the effectiveness of plug fishing. Trolling with crankbaits, minnowbaits and vibrating plugs is one of the hottest tournament techniques, especially on big water.

Plugs enable you to cover a lot of water in a hurry, a big advantage when you're working highly mobile schools of fish suspended in open water.

To increase their horizontal and vertical coverage, anglers often troll with side planers and weight their lines differently. Some even use lead-core line, downriggers and 3-way swivel rigs.

But plugs are also effective for casting, especially when the fish move into the shallows in the evening. When the water is cool, a neutrally-buoyant minnowbait works especially well, because you can stop reeling and "hang" it right in their faces.

Big walleyes love minnowbaits!

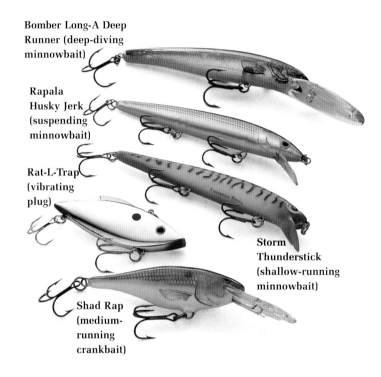

Bomber Long-A Deep Runner (deep-diving minnowbait)

Rapala Husky Jerk (suspending minnowbait)

Rat-L-Trap (vibrating plug)

Storm Thunderstick (shallow-running minnowbait)

Shad Rap (medium-running crankbait)

Plug-Fishing Tips

Side planers make it possible to cover a lot of water and, because your lines are far to the side of the boat, you're not as likely to spook the fish.

Cast a minnowbait over rocky shoals starting at sunset. The fish move in to feed on minnows and are often caught in water less than 5 feet deep.

Ice Fishing

Like most coolwater fish, walleyes and saugers continue to feed at near-freezing temperatures, so they're a prime target for ice fishermen. Although you can catch them throughout the winter, the fastest action tends to be early and late in the ice-cover season.

As a rule, the spots that produced fish in summer and fall will continue to produce after freeze up. If you have a handheld GPS unit, you can easily return to a waypoint entered during the open-water season.

A minnow dangled beneath a tip-up or bobber accounts for plenty of walleyes and saugers, but jigging is even more productive. Not only does the jigging action attract more fish, you can move about more easily because you don't have to reset your depth every time you switch holes.

One of the best ways to locate walleyes and saugers is to drill at least a dozen holes, all at different depths, then set out tip-ups in some of the holes and jig in the others. If you start catching fish in a certain area or at a certain depth, move the rest of your lines accordingly.

If the fish don't bite in an hour or so, try another spot; it normally doesn't pay to wait them out.

Whatever technique you use, be sure to arrive at your ice-fishing spot well before you expect the fish to start biting. If they normally bite at dusk, for instance, start drilling your holes in late afternoon. If you wait until the fish are feeding to start drilling holes, the sound of the auger may put an end to the action.

A good flasher not only tells you what depth the fish are at, it shows you how they react to different jigging actions.

Swedish Pimple with minnow head

Jigging Rapala

Fireball Jig tipped with rear half of minnow

A good jigging outfit includes a fast-action graphite rod about 30 inches long with at least 3 guides and a fly-rod-style tip, a small spinning reel that balances with the rod, and limp 6-pound-test mono.

WHITE & STRIPED BASS

Morone chrysops & Morone saxatilis

These super-aggressive feeders offer some of the fastest freshwater fishing – if you can find them. Both species are known for their pelagic habits, spending a good deal of their time chasing baitfish in open water.

White and striped bass belong to the temperate bass family and are not related to the largemouth or other black bass. Other members of the family include white perch and yellow bass.

Hybrids can be produced by crossing male white bass and female striped bass. Called wipers, these popular fish are stocked in many southern waters.

White bass are also known as "sand bass" or "silver bass," and striped bass are often called "rockfish." The name "striper" often leads to confusion, because it may be applied to both species.

White & Striped Bass Facts

Although white and striped bass are closely relat-ed, white bass spend their entire life in fresh water, while striped bass are anadromous, spending most of their life at sea and enter-ing freshwater streams to spawn. But striped bass are capable of living solely in fresh water and have been widely stocked, mainly in southern reservoirs.

White and striped bass are warmwater gamefish, prefer-ring water temperatures from the mid 60s to the mid 70s. White bass thrive in big-river systems, including

White bass range.

Striped bass range.

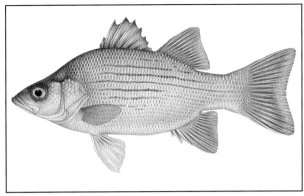

White bass have silvery sides with black horizontal stripes that are usually unbroken above the lateral line but broken below.

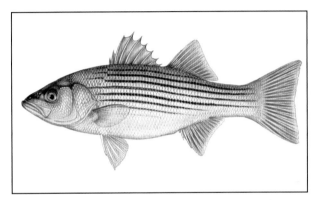

Striped bass have silvery sides with 7 or 8 horizontal stripes that are unbroken. The body is more elongated than that of a white bass.

connecting lakes. Striped bass are well suited to large reservoirs with an ample supply of open-water forage, usually shad.

Both white and striped bass spawn in spring, generally at water temperatures in the mid 50s to low 60s. They swim up tributary streams, usually until their progress is blocked by a dam, and then deposit their eggs in light current. They make no attempt to guard the eggs.

Fish make up most of the diet, but both species also eat crustaceans and a variety of aquatic insects. They are known for their pack-feeding behavior. When a hun-gry pack surrounds a school of baitfish, you'll witness a feeding frenzy more explosive than anything else you'll ever see in fresh water. They herd the baitfish to the surface, slashing at them from below, while gulls and terns dive down to grab those that get injured in the melee. Anglers lucky enough to encounter a feeding pack often catch a fish on every cast. But the action is usually short-lived, especially when boats get too close. The pack sounds, but may soon reappear in a different location.

Striped bass grow much faster and live much longer than white bass. In 5 years, a white bass normally grows to about 1½ pounds; a striper, about 10 pounds. White bass seldom live longer than 6 years, while stripers may reach an age of 20 or more.

Striped bass grow to a larger size in salt water than in fresh water. Commercial fishermen off the Atlantic coast once netted a striped bass that weighed 125 pounds.

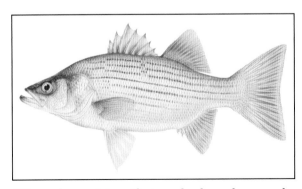

Wipers have stripes that are broken above and sometimes below the lateral line. The body is deeper than that of a striper but not as deep as a white bass.

Key Locations for White and Striped Bass...

In Man-Made Lakes

Early Spring through Spawning:
- Tailwaters of upstream dams
- Creek arms at the upper end of the lake, particularly those with a significant flow

Tailwaters

Late Spring through Mid-Fall:
- Edges of shallow flats
- Mouths of major creek arms
- Suspended over the old river channel and creek channels or in the submerged timber along the edges
- Edges of shallow main-lake points
- Narrows between main-lake basins

Late Fall and Winter:
- Coves between main-lake points
- Junction of creek channel and old river channel
- Deep holes in the old river channel at the lower end of the lake (late fall to early winter)
- Deep holes in the old river channel at the upper end of the lake (late winter)
- Deep main lake points, especially those at the upper end of the lake

Deep point extending into river channel

In Rivers

Early Spring through Spawning:
- Large backwaters that warm earlier than the main river
- Tailwaters of upstream dams
- Mouths of large tributaries

Tributaries carry warmer water that draws spawners

Late Spring through Mid-Fall:
- Sandy flats around mouths of tributaries
- Pools with rocky feeding riffle just upstream
- Deep riprap banks along outside bends
- Slots and washouts below boulders and other large objects that break the current
- Eddies created by sharp turns in the river
- Eddies created by points projecting into the river

Deep pool below rocky riffle

Late Fall and Winter:
- Deepest pools in the river
- Holes along outside bends
- Deep washouts in the tailwaters of upstream dams

Fishing for Temperate Bass

The secret to catching temperate bass is finding them. White bass, striped bass and wipers are constantly on the move, and the spot that held a huge school yesterday may not produce a single fish today.

Finding the fish is easiest in spring, when they congregate below dams to spawn. But once they complete spawning and move back downstream or into a lake, locating them can be a challenge. That's when most anglers rely on trolling so they can cover lots of water.

The fish begin their pack-feeding behavior in late summer or early fall. Then, circling gulls will help you pinpoint feeding schools.

As a rule, temperate bass bite best early and late in the day but, during the spawning period, time of day is not much of a consideration. The action slows considerably when the water temperature drops below 50°F, although white bass are often caught by ice fishermen.

You can use similar techniques to catch white and striped bass, but the latter require bigger lures and heavier tackle. Live bait, however, is seldom necessary for white bass.

Recommended Tackle

A light- to medium-power spinning outfit with 4- to 8-pound mono is adequate for most types of white bass fishing. A medium-heavy- to heavy-power baitcasting outfit with 14- to 25-pound mono is a good choice for striped bass.

Trolling

Trolling for temperate bass can be as simple as tossing a jig or crankbait behind the boat or as complicated as rigging 6 or 8 lines on planer boards and downriggers to cover a wider, deeper swath of water.

Live shad are the favorite trolling bait of many striped bass anglers. Hook them through the nostrils and use an electric trolling motor to move them along very slowly. Watch your depth finder for signs of fish or baitfish schools, and set your lines to fish just above them.

Jigs and plugs can be trolled much faster, so they're a better choice when you're searching for fish.

Should you find a good-sized school of fish, stop the boat and try casting or vertical jigging. Not only will you cover the area more thoroughly, you'll be much less likely to spook the fish.

For Stripers

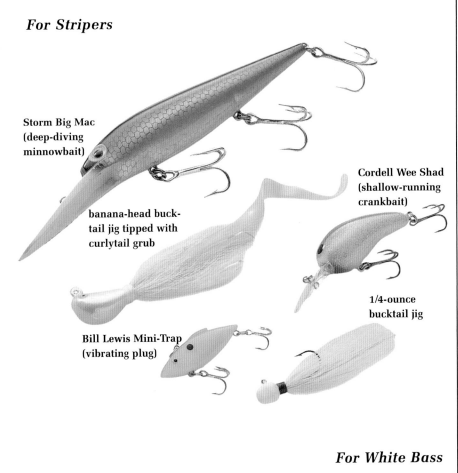

Storm Big Mac (deep-diving minnowbait)

banana-head bucktail jig tipped with curlytail grub

Cordell Wee Shad (shallow-running crankbait)

Bill Lewis Mini-Trap (vibrating plug)

1/4-ounce bucktail jig

For White Bass

Circling gulls lead you to feeding white bass and stripers.

Jump-Fishing

In late summer, when young-of-the-year shad have grown large enough to make a decent meal, white bass and stripers begin pack-feeding. If you watch closely for circling and diving gulls, they'll lead you to the fish.

To some, the term "jump-fishing" means anglers jumping from school to school; to others, it means fish jumping bait. Either way, jump-fishing provides incredible action. Just toss out any bait that looks even remotely like a shad and there's a good chance you'll hook up immediately.

Veteran jump-fishermen rely mainly on jigs, because they can unhook the fish and get back into the water in a hurry. That's important, because the action may not last long, especially if you get your boat too close to the school. Some white bass anglers use a tandem-jig set-up (right), so they can catch two fish at a time.

But there are times when crankbaits, tail-spinners or topwaters work better than jigs. Striped bass anglers know that a big, noisy popper, one that throws water a foot into the air, often draws strikes when nothing else is working.

For Stripers

Cordell Redfin (shallow-running minnowbait)

Creek Chub Striper Strike (chugger)

Roadrunner Jig tipped with paddletail worm

Pop-R Plus (chugger)

Little George (tailspinner)

Tandem jig setup

For White Bass

A lively shad can easily tow a high-floating balloon.

Balloon Fishing

Big striped bass have a penchant for heavy cover; they often hole up in flooded timber or other cover where it's virtually impossible to throw a lure. But southern striper guides have devised an innovative method for drawing them out of the tangle. They hook on a live, 12- to 15-inch shad and let it swim enticingly over the cover, using a balloon as a float.

A balloon works much better than a bobber. Because it floats considerably higher, it has less water resistance, so a lively shad can tow it around more easily and cover more water.

If the balloon breaks or starts bobbing violently, a striper has taken the bait. Reel up slack until you feel the weight of the fish and set the hook hard. Keep maximum pressure on the fish to keep it from diving.

The major challenge in balloon fishing is collecting the shad. You can't buy them at a bait shop, so you'll have to net your own. Serious striper fishermen catch their bait with a cast net and keep it alive in an aerated, insulated bait tank.

When you're fishing stripers in timber or other dense cover, heavy tackle is a must. When you hook a big fish, it invariably makes a power run for the thickest cover and, if you're not able to turn it immediately, you have little chance of landing it. Many anglers use a light saltwater rod and a heavy baitcasting reel spooled with 50-pound-test mono or superline.

Inflate a small balloon to a diameter of 4 or 5 inches, stretch out the neck and tie a single overhand knot around your line. Set the balloon to the desired depth.

Push a size 3/0 to 6/0 hook through shad's lips or nostrils, or hook it just in front of the dorsal fin. Don't attach a sinker; it will restrict the shad's movement.

STREAM TROUT

The term "stream trout" refers to species of trout that require moving water for successful spawning. Stream trout are also found in lakes, if there is a suitable tributary stream available for spawning. If not, they must be stocked.

The major stream-trout species include brown, rainbow, cutthroat and brook trout. The latter is actually a char and is more closely related to the lake trout than to the other stream trout. Char are easy to distinguish from trout because they have light spots on a dark background; trout have dark spots on a light background.

Stream Trout Facts

Stream trout are coldwater fish. Whether they inhabit streams or lakes, they require water that stays cold and well-oxygenated throughout the year.

Brook trout, like other chars, need very cold water; they prefer a water temperature of about 54°F. Brown trout can tolerate relatively warm water. They favor a water temperature of about 65°F, but can endure temperatures in the upper 70s. Rainbow and cutthroat have intermediate temperature preferences.

All of these stream trout species develop *anadromous*, or seagoing, varieties. The best known of these is the steelhead, a variety of rainbow trout that spends most of its life at sea and then enters coastal streams to spawn. Anadromous forms are usually sleeker and more silvery than their landlocked counterparts.

Steelhead and other anadromous stream trout have been stocked in large inland lakes, particularly the Great Lakes. There, the fish spend most of their lives in the open waters of the lakes, and run up tributary streams to spawn.

Rainbows and cutthroats are spring spawners, while browns and brooks spawn in fall. All stream trout build *redds*, depressions in the streambed gravel into which the eggs are deposited. The eggs are then covered with gravel and allowed to incubate. Water must flow through the gravel to keep the eggs aerated, explaining why stream trout cannot spawn successfully in lakes. The parents do not protect the redd or guard the young.

Aquatic insects, including both larval and adult forms, are an important food source for all stream trout. But as the trout grow older, small fish make up

Brook trout range.

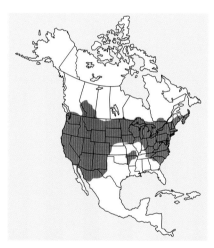

Brown trout range.

Brook trout (Salvelinus fontinalis), also called speckled trout, have brownish to greenish sides with light spots and a few red spots with blue halos. The back has light wormlike markings and the leading edges of the lower fins are white.

Brown trout (Salmo trutta) have light brownish or yellowish sides with black spots along with a few red or orange spots. The spots sometimes have lighter halos. The tail is usually unspotted, but it may have a few spots.

a larger portion of their diet. Fish are especially important in the diet of large brown trout. Other stream trout foods include crustaceans, worms, frogs, plankton and fish eggs.

Stream trout are known for their selective feeding habits, explaining why fly fishermen take great pains to "match the hatch." But selectivity varies greatly among species, with browns being by far the most choosy. Rainbows are less selective, while brook trout and cutthroat will take most anything you throw at them.

Stream trout are not particularly long-lived. The maximum life span is 8 to 10 years, although brook trout have been known to live 15 years. Growth is extremely variable. As a rule, lake-dwelling and anadromous forms grow much faster and reach a considerably larger size than stream-dwelling forms. Male stream trout generally grow faster than females.

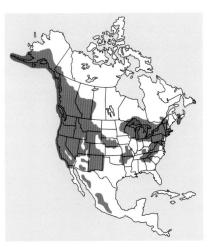

Rainbow trout range.

Cutthroat trout range.

Rainbow trout (Oncorhynchus mykiss) have a bluish or greenish back and silvery sides with a pinkish horizontal band that extends over the gill cover. The back, sides and tail are heavily spotted.

Cutthroat trout (Oncorhynchus clarki) get their name from the orange or red slash marks on the throat. The sides usually have a yellowish tinge, with black spots. The tail is heavily spotted.

Fishing for Stream Trout

Hundreds of books have been written about techniques for outwitting stream trout. But regardless of what method you use, there are several common threads:

• Don't let the fish see or hear you. That means keeping a low profile, wearing drab clothing and keeping movement to a minimum. If you're wading, move slowly and silently. If you're in a boat, don't drop anything on the bottom or run the motor anywhere near the fish. If you're walking along the bank, use streamside vegetation to conceal your approach, and step lightly to minimize vibrations. And never allow your shadow to fall over a potential lie. Once the fish detect you, no amount of coaxing will convince them to bite.

• Use a delicate presentation. If your lure or line splashes down near the fish, they'll head for cover.

• Use a light, low-visibility leader or tippet, because trout are extremely line-shy. Never use fluorescent mono.

• When a major insect hatch is in progress, small-to medium-size trout feed almost exclusively on the hatching insect, and the only effective way to catch them is fishing with a fly of the same size, shape and color. But the biggest trout are usually more interested in baitfish than insects, so they're susceptible to lures such as spinners, spoons, minnowbaits and streamers.

Key Locations for Stream Trout...

In Streams

• Gravelly tributaries or gravelly tails of pools serve as spawning sites for rainbows and cutthroats
• Riffles (shallow, turbulent water) hold feeding trout in morning and evening
• Runs (deep channels excavated by the current), hold trout most anytime
• Pools (deep, flat water) are ideal resting areas. They often hold the stream's biggest trout
• Undercut banks offer shade and overhead cover
• Spring holes in the headwaters (brook trout)
• Spring areas draw trout during the hottest part of the summer (marginal trout streams)
• Plunge pools that form at the base of a waterfall are prime spots for big trout
• "Pocket water" (scattered boulders on shallow flats with pockets of deep water behind them) holds a surprising number of trout
• Gravelly reaches near the headwaters and gravelly tributaries draw spawning brook and brown trout in fall

Undercuts often form along outside bends

In Lakes

• Shallow bays warm earlier than the main body of a lake, so they attract trout in early spring
• Shorelines with a gradual taper are prime spots in deep, cold lakes
• Rocky points with a slow taper make good morning and evening feeding sites
• Inlet streams carry an abundance of food and draw good numbers of trout

Look for trout around weedy or brushy cover

• Cool water in the thermocline may hold practically all the trout in mid-summer, when the surface water is too warm for trout and the depths have too little oxygen
• Weedy or woody cover is a must for trout in shallow water; otherwise, the fish would be vulnerable to kingfishers, herons and other predators

---

Recommended Tackle

A light- to medium power spinning outfit with 4- to 8-pound mono is adequate for fishing with spoons, spinners and other "hardware."

A 3- to 5-weight fly rod, a double-taper or weight-forward line and a 9-foot tapered leader with a 5X to 6X tippet is suitable for the majority of stream-trout fishing. But if you're casting big flies or fishing for good-sized trout in fast water or heavy cover, you'll need a 7- to 9-weight fly rod and a 0X to 4X tippet.

to stand downstream of a riffle where you suspect trout are feeding, cast upstream of the riffle and crank the lure rapidly through it.

Medium- to deep-diving crankbaits are a good choice for fishing deep pools or trolling for suspended trout in lakes.

Lake fishermen often use side planers to spread their lines and catch trout that spook from the boat. They also use downriggers and diving planes to take their lures to the desired depth (pp. 40-41).

When stream-fishing, quarter your casts upstream far enough that you don't have to retrieve against the current (red line). If you cast too far downstream, the current will catch your line, forming a belly, speeding up the lure and causing you to retrieve upstream (yellow line).

Fishing with Hardware

The vast majority of trophy-class stream trout are taken on "hardware," primarily spinners, spoons, and plugs. That should come as no surprise, because these lures imitate baitfish, the favorite food of big trout.

Spinners are popular among both stream and lake fishermen, because they produce a lot of flash and vibration, even on a very slow retrieve. You can reel them rapidly through a fast riffle or slow them way down to fish a deep pool.

Heavy spoons are ideal for distance casting on big water, and they have enough weight to get down in fast current. But thinner spoons have more action and work better for trolling.

Minnowbaits are more difficult to cast, but their lifelike appearance appeals to selective trout. One of the best ways to fish a minnowbait is

Luhr Jensen Flutter Spoon

Rebel Ghost (minnowbait)

Fat Rap (shallow-running crankbait)

Krocodile Spoon

Mepps Spinner

Fly Fishing

Fly fishing for trout is the passion of millions of anglers. For some, learning to make perfect casts with a fly line is the source of fascination; for others, it's tying flies that match natural insect hatches. Many consider fly fishing an art form, but it's also an extremely effective way to catch trout.

Flies can be tied to match most anything that a trout eats, but the majority of flies imitate larval or adult forms of aquatic insects.

Dry flies mimic newly-hatched adult insects. Many have upright hair or feather wings. A collar of feather fibers, or *hackle*, along with a hair or feather tail, gives the fly buoyancy, but it must be periodically dipped in floatant to keep it from sinking. Dry flies are fished on a dead drift.

Wet flies imitate many different trout foods, including larval aquatic insects, drowned terrestrial insects, minnows and crustaceans. Most wet flies have swept-back wings and are intended to sink. Wet flies can be fished on a dead drift or twitched to resemble a darting minnow or insect.

Nymphs usually simulate the nymphal, larval or pupal stages of aquatic insects, but some patterns imitate scuds, shrimp and other crustaceans. They are tied on heavy hooks and fished beneath the surface on a dead drift. Some are weighted so they can be fished on the bottom.

Streamers are tied on extra-long hooks and have long hair or feather wings to make them resemble minnows. They are fished beneath the surface with long strips to mimic a darting baitfish.

Popular Trout Flies

Royal Coachman (wet)

Hare's Ear (nymph)

Adams (dry)

Matuka (streamer)

Fishing Dry Flies

Cast the fly upstream, either straight or at an angle. Let it float naturally downstream.

Strip in slack line as the fly drifts toward you, but do not disturb the natural drift.

If a belly develops, mend the line by flipping it upstream. Otherwise, the current causes drag on the fly.

Fishing Streamers & Wet Flies

Hold the fly line under a finger of your rod hand while stripping line with your other hand. Let excess fly line fall to the water. Experiment with different strip lengths to find the right action. Wet flies are usually fished with shorter strips than are streamers.

Fishing Nymphs

Angle your cast upstream and strip in slack to keep the line tight as the fly drifts. Otherwise, you won't feel the strike. If desired, use a strike indicator (inset).

If necessary, add a small split shot to keep your nymph on the bottom. Don't use too much weight, however, or the fly will hang up.

Bait Fishing

With their highly developed sense of smell, trout can easily detect natural bait, even in water too murky for flies or hardware.

Natural bait is also a good choice in early spring, when the water is cold and very few insects are hatching.

Garden worms, nightcrawlers and salmon eggs are the most popular natural baits but, in some areas, anglers rely heavily on minnows, cut bait, leeches, crayfish, grasshoppers, crickets and aquatic insects, both larval and adult.

"Grocery baits," such as corn and marshmallows, prepared baits that mold onto the hook and soft plastics impregnated with scent also work well, particularly for freshly stocked trout.

You can fish natural bait beneath a small float, attach a sinker and still-fish it on the bottom or weight it lightly so it tumbles along the bottom at the same speed as the current. The latter presentation is most realistic and enables you to cover the greatest amount of water.

Popular Baits for Stream Trout

(1) Garden worm, *(2)* nightcrawler, *(3)* mayfly nymph, *(4)* grasshopper, *(5)* single salmon egg, *(6)* kernel of corn, *(7)* marshmallow.

It takes a sturdy jigging rod to land trout like this.

Jigging Rapala

Little Cleo Spoon

icefly tipped with waxworm

Fat Boy jig tipped with Eurolarvae

Ice Fishing

Ice fishing for stream trout is much like ice fishing for sunfish and crappies. You can use the same kinds of lures, but you may need a little heavier tackle, because trout fight especially hard in the frigid water.

Mobility is the key to success with most types of ice fishing, and it's no different with stream trout. Anglers drill lots of holes and use jigging techniques that enable them to move about easily. A depth finder is a must, because trout frequently suspend well off the bottom.

Popular jigging baits include swimming minnows and teardrops or small jigging spoons tipped with waxworms, Eurolarvae, scuds or pieces of red worm.

A medium-power graphite jigging rod, about 30 inches long, is ideal for jigging stream trout. Pair it with a small spinning reel that has a smooth drag, and spool up with 4- to 6-pound-test clear monofilament.

LAKE TROUT

Salvelinus namaycush

Lake trout are truly "denizens of the deep." "Lakers," also called gray trout and mackinaw, require very cold water, so they are commonly found in depths of 50 to 100 feet and may be considerably deeper. Their preferred temperature range is 48 to 52°F, lower than that of any other freshwater gamefish.

But lakers are not always found in deep water. In very large lakes, such as Lake Superior, they're commonly caught on the surface, even in summer, because the water temperature is within their comfort zone.

Lake trout may be crossed with brook trout to produce a hybrid called the *splake*. These fish are sometimes stocked in infertile northern lakes.

Lake Trout Facts

Lake trout are found primarily in deep, infertile lakes. Shallow lakes, unless they are located in the Arctic, do not have cold enough water. And fertile lakes, even if they are deep, do not have adequate dissolved oxygen in the depths.

Lakers spawn in the fall, usually at water temperatures in the upper 40s or low 50s. They deposit their eggs on rocky reefs from a few feet to more than 30 feet deep. The eggs fall into crevices in the rocks, where they can incubate safe from predators until they hatch in spring. Lake trout spawn on the same reefs each year.

In most waters, the lake trout's diet consists mainly of fish. They commonly eat cold-water species, such as ciscoes, whitefish, smelt and burbot, but they will take whatever is available. In lakes where forage fish are scarce, lakers feed on plankton, crustaceans and insects. But, in this situation, they rarely grow larger than two or three pounds.

The feeding habits of lake trout are unusual in that they can move up and down considerable distances in the water to find food. A laker in 80 feet of water, for instance, can easily swim up 50 feet to take ciscoes suspended in the thermocline. They compensate for water pressure changes by burping up air through a duct connecting their swim bladder to their esophagus.

Lake trout grow very slowly, but may live as long as 40 years. Typically, it takes about 11 years for a lake trout to reach 5 pounds and, in the Far North, where

Lake trout range.

Key Locations for Lake Trout...

Early Spring:
- Off slow-tapering shorelines and islands
- Ends of gradually sloping rocky points
- Narrows between two basins of the main lake

Trout like the steep breaks that cliff walls provide

Narrows make a natural funnel

Summer and Early Fall:
- Sharp-breaking lips of islands and points
- Deep humps
- Deep slots and holes in an otherwise shallow part of the lake

- Off steep cliff walls

Mid-Fall through Spawning:
- Shallow, flat-topped reefs
- Shallow, rocky points with long extended lips
- Shallow, rocky shelves along shorelines and islands

Winter:
- Same structure that held trout in summer, although the fish may be shallower

the growing season is extremely short, it may take twice that long.

Nevertheless, lake trout reach astonishing sizes. In northern Canada and a few large lakes in the western states, 30- to 40-pound lakers are fairly common and anglers take an occasional giant exceeding 50 pounds. The

biggest lake trout on record was netted in Saskatchewan's Lake Athabasca. It weighed 102 pounds.

The extremely slow growth of the lake trout means that fishing regulations must be quite restrictive to prevent overharvest. Bag limits are generally low and open seasons, relatively short.

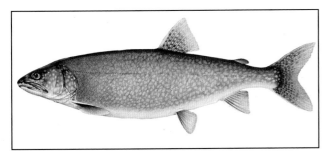

Lake trout have light spots on a greenish to grayish background, and a deeply forked tail. The lower fins have white leading edges.

Splake resemble lake trout, but they have the brook trout's worm-like markings on the back, and the tail is not as deeply forked.

Fishing for Lake Trout

Anglers use a wide array of techniques to catch lake trout, depending mainly on depth of the water.

When the fish go deep in summer, you can reach them with downriggers, by deep-trolling with 3-way rigs or by vertical jigging.

When they're shallow, try casting or long-line trolling with spoons or plugs, or still-fishing with dead bait, such as a smelt, cisco or chunk of sucker meat.

Recommended Tackle

Medium- to medium-heavy-power spinning or baitcasting gear with 8- to 14-pound-test mono is adequate for most types of lake trout fishing. But with superline, about 30-pound-test works better for vertical jigging or trolling with a 3-way rig. Because it has no stretch, you can feel strikes better in deep water and get a much stronger hookset.

Lake trout are usually taken in water that is relatively snag-free, so there is no need for extremely heavy tackle. Lakers, like stream trout, are quite line-shy, and heavy line will reduce the number of strikes you get.

Downriggers give you precise depth control. When you see the fish on your graph, lower the cannonball to keep your bait tracking just above them.

Popular Vertical Jigging & Trolling Baits

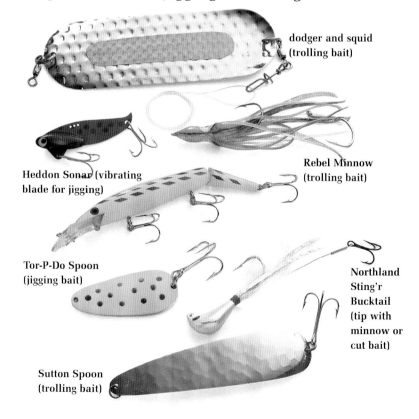

dodger and squid (trolling bait)

Heddon Sonar (vibrating blade for jigging)

Rebel Minnow (trolling bait)

Tor-P-Do Spoon (jigging bait)

Northland Sting'r Bucktail (tip with minnow or cut bait)

Sutton Spoon (trolling bait)

Other Lake Trout Techniques

Vertical jigging with a 1- to 2-ounce lead-head jig or jigging spoon enables you to work deep lake trout schools that you've located with your graph. Lift the lure with long sweeps of the rod, keeping the line taut as the lure sinks.

Trolling with a 3-way-rig (inset) is an excellent big-trout method. The larger the trout, the less susceptible they are to vertical jigging. They would rather lie close to the bottom and grab a lure trolled at their level.

A 3-foot, medium-heavy-power jigging rod and a baitcasting reel spooled with 20-pound-test superline make an ideal outfit for jigging lake trout through the ice.

Ice Fishing

Because of their preference for frigid water, lake trout stay active all winter and are relatively easy to catch by ice fishing. And they're found in pretty much the same areas you would find them in summer.

The two main methods used by ice anglers are jigging and tip-up fishing. Where multiple lines are legal, set out one or more tip-ups baited with live or dead baitfish, and jig with another line. When the fish are active, they'll hit the jig; when they're not, tip-ups usually work better.

Popular Ice-Jigging Lures

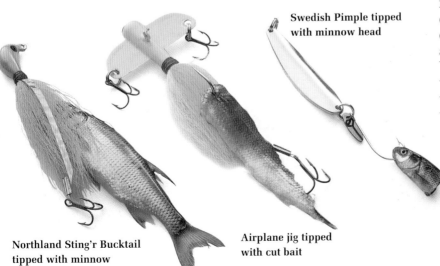

Swedish Pimple tipped with minnow head

Northland Sting'r Bucktail tipped with minnow

Airplane jig tipped with cut bait

SALMON

Thanks to massive stockings of Pacific salmon in the Great Lakes and the prairie reservoirs of the Dakotas, you no longer have to travel to Alaska or the Pacific Northwest to tangle with these world-class fighters.

Because salmon are anadromous fish, they can survive in fresh as well as salt water. When stocked in fresh water, salmon spend most of their life roaming the vast expanses of inland lakes, just as they as they would roam about at sea. And just as saltwater salmon spawn in coastal streams, freshwater salmon spawn (or attempt to) in streams flowing into the big lakes.

Of the five species of Pacific salmon (chinook, coho, pink, sockeye and chum), the chinook and coho have been stocked most widely in fresh water. Chinooks are also called king salmon and cohos, silver salmon.

Sea-run Atlantic salmon, considered one of the world's premier gamefish, enter streams along the North Atlantic Coast, mainly in Canada. Landlocked Atlantic salmon have been widely stocked, primarily in the New England states.

Salmon Facts.

All salmon are coldwater fish, preferring water temperatures in the low to upper 50s. They go wherever they must to find temperatures in this range, swimming across miles of open water or drastically changing depths as temperatures change because of wind or current.

Small fish make up most of the diet of chinooks and cohos. In the Great Lakes, they feed mainly on alewives; in the Dakota reservoirs, smelt. Atlantics and land-locks feed primarily on insects and crustaceans, although they may eat small fish as well.

All species of salmon spawn in the fall. They ascend tributary streams, often jumping high falls and wiggling their way through shallow riffles until they find a gravelly spawning shoal that suits them. They deposit their eggs in redds in the same manner as stream trout. Spawning in tributaries of

Chinook salmon range.

Coho salmon range.

Chinook salmon (Oncorhynchus tshawytscha) have silvery sides with dark spots on the back. Both lobes of the tail are spotted. The anal fin is considerably longer than it is deep. The teeth are set in black gums.

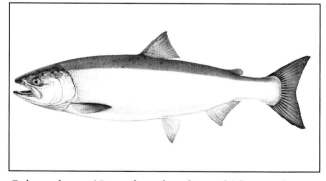

Coho salmon (Oncorhynchus kisutch) have silvery sides with dark spots on the back, but only the upper lobe of the tail is spotted. The anal fin is about as long as it is deep, and the teeth are set in whitish gums.

fixed life cycle, so they continue to feed during their spawning run. They may live as long as 10 years.

The chinook is the largest salmon species. In Alaska, sea-run chinook commonly reach weights of 50 to 60 pounds in 4 years. In the Great Lakes, chinooks over 30 pounds are unusual. Sea-run cohos grow only slightly faster than cohos in the Great lakes. In fact, the world-record coho was taken in a Lake Ontario tributary. Sea-run Atlantic salmon grow much faster than landlocks. A typical sea-run Atlantic reaches a weight of 25 pounds in 6 years; a landlock grows to only 5 pounds in that time.

Atlantic salmon range.

inland lakes is not often successful, although reproduction of chinooks and cohos has been documented in the Great Lakes.

Pacific salmon have a fixed life cycle, meaning that they live a certain number of years, then spawn and die. Chinooks generally spawn at age 4; cohos, age 3. Prior to spawning, the fish change color, usually turning pink, red or olive, and their flesh begins to deteriorate. They do not feed once they begin their spawning run, although they may strike lures out of aggression.

Atlantic salmon do not have a

Sea-run Atlantic salmon (salmo salar) have silvery to yellowish-brown sides with irregular X- or Y-shaped black marks. They often resemble brown trout, but the tail is slightly forked and the adipose fin is unspotted.

Fishing for Salmon

Despite the fact that Pacific salmon are highly aggressive feeders, triggering them to strike may be a challenge, especially as spawning time approaches. By the time they begin to congregate around the mouths of spawning streams, their digestive tract has already started to deteriorate and they are striking mainly out of aggression.

Even before feeding slows, the fish can be highly selective. They're known for their tendency to pick out a particular bait in a certain color, to the exclusion of everything else. Then, a day or two later, they want something completely different.

Salmon are sensitive to sunlight, explaining why they do their heaviest feeding early and late in the day. Most anglers agree that early morning is best; in fact; you'll often catch more fish during the first hour of daylight than you will the rest of the day.

Salmon often feed in shallow water close to shore in the morning but, as the sun rises higher, they usually move to deeper water, sometimes several miles away from shore.

Because salmon are so sensitive to changes in water temperature, open-water anglers pay close attention to the wind. When an offshore wind blows the warm surface water away from shore, and cold water from the depths wells up to replace it, salmon move closer to shore and are often caught by anglers casting from piers and breakwaters. But when the wind blows in, warm water piles up along shore and the salmon move out.

Trolling is, by far, the most productive method for catching Pacific or landlocked-salmon in open water. You can use downriggers and planer boards to spread your lines vertically and horizontally, greatly increasing your area of coverage.

Once fish enter the streams, you can cast for them with spoons and spinners or drift-fish with yarn flies or fresh spawn.

Recommended Tackle

Medium-heavy-power spinning or baitcasting gear with 12- to 20-pound-test monofilament is suitable for the majority of salmon fishing.

Downrigger fishermen use slow-action rods, about 8- to 8$^1/_2$- feet in length. There is no need for sensitivity in downrigger fishing, and the long, soft rod helps cushion the fight, minimizing line breakage.

Key Locations for Salmon . . .

Large numbers of salmon gather around stream mouths prior to spawning.

In Lakes
- Edges of deep shoreline shelves
- Deep humps
- Deep edges of long, gradually tapering points
- Stream mouths
- Off steep cliff faces

- Suspended wherever the water temperature is in the mid 50s
- Along surface temperature breaks between warm and cold water
- Around baitfish schools

Great Lakes salmon often congregate in deep water off steep cliffs in summer.

In Rivers
- Deep pools
- Deep slots along outside bends
- Shallow riffles (spawning)
- Tails of pools (spawning)

Tails of pools are popular fishing spots.

Salmon Fishing Tips

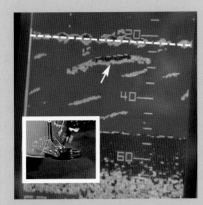

Adjust your transducer by tipping it back slightly (inset) so your graph picks up your cannonballs. Then, you can easily keep your lures tracking just above the fish.

Set downrigger rods with enough tension so they bend into a deep arc. Then, when a fish strikes and the line releases, the rod will stand up straight to signal a strike before the fish removes all the slack.

Downrigger Fishing

Downriggers greatly improve your trolling efficiency. Not only do they enable you to precisely control your depth, they make it possible to spread lines at various levels.

But, most importantly, they allow you to fish in deep water without a heavy weight on your line to take away from the enjoyment of fighting the fish. An 8- to 12-pound cannonball attached to a steel cable takes your line to the desired depth. When a fish strikes, your line releases from the cable and you can fight the fish with no weight to interfere.

To run lines at different levels, simply use several downriggers, or rig a single downrigger with *stackers,* release devices that attach to the downrigger cable. Stackers enable you to run as many as three lines off the same downrigger but, if the release holding your bottom line trips, you'll have to reset all the lines.

A good graph is a big help in downrigger fishing. It will show you how deep the fish are running, so you can set your lines accordingly. And, if the transducer is aimed properly, you can see your cannonballs, so you're sure they're in the fish zone.

Popular Downrigger Baits

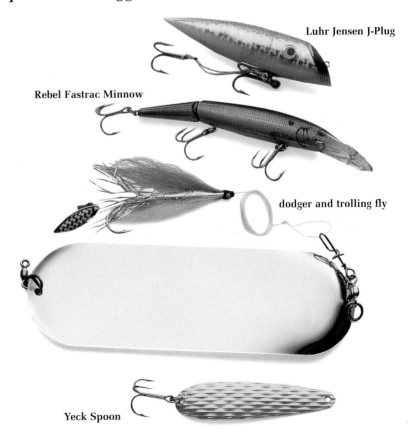

Luhr Jensen J-Plug

Rebel Fastrac Minnow

dodger and trolling fly

Yeck Spoon

Trolling boards allow you to run your baits far to the side of the boat's wake. Some anglers use two or even three lines spaced along the cord going to each board, so you can thoroughly cover a wide swath of water.

Fishing with "Boards"

When salmon are in shallow water or holding close to the surface, they're likely to spook from the boat when you troll over them. But you can solve the problem by using trolling boards or side planers to spread your lines. Use the same lures as you would in downrigger fishing.

Trolling boards plane up to 75 feet to the side of the boat, meaning that lines can be spread more than 150 feet apart. Your lines attach to the cord with releases much like those used for downrigger fishing. When a fish strikes, you can fight it on a free line.

Side planers (p.41) do not pull as far to the side as trolling boards. Because they stay on your line while you're landing the fish, they not only detract from the fight, they drag in the water

and increase the chances that you'll lose the fish.

In rough water, trolling boards work better than side planers, because they're less likely to tip over or skip in the waves. Double boards are even more stable than single ones.

How to Use Trolling Boards

After letting out the board, let your fishing line out the desired distance. Clip the line to a release and let it slide down the cord to within a foot or so of the board. Engage the reel to keep the line from sliding farther, and place the rod in a rod holder.

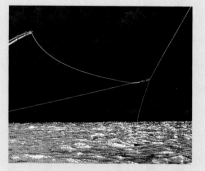

Let out another line and clip it to a release. Let the second release slide halfway down the cord and then stop it by engaging the reel. Set the rod in a rod holder. Repeat the procedure to set a pair of lines on the opposite side of the boat.

Stream Fishing

The sheer numbers of salmon jammed into a stream during the spawning run explain why stream fishing can be outstanding, even when the fish are not feeding.

Nobody really knows why spawning Pacific salmon bite when their digestive tract is deteriorating. Some suspect it's a reflex action; others say they're protecting their territory. Whatever the reason, they'll hit flashy baits, such as spoons and spinners, as well as spawn bags and yarn flies.

Casting with spoons and spinners works best when salmon are scattered over large areas of the stream. Be sure to quarter your casts upstream far enough that the lure gets down to the bottom, because that's where most of the fish are.

When salmon are holding in specific runs or near redds, try drift-fishing with yarn flies or spawn bags. Be sure to use a long rod, at least 8½ feet, so you can keep most of the line out of the water and control the bait in the current. With a rod this long, there is no need to cast; simply work the spot by repeatedly picking up the bait and flicking it back upstream.

Pixie Spoon

Vibrax spinner

spawn bag

yarn fly

Luhr-Jensen Hotshot

INDEX

3 0646 00239 7085

RIVERHEAD FREE LIBRARY
330 COURT ST
RIVERHEAD, NY 11901